HINTS 4 HAPPINESS

Copyright © 2023 by mOjAf.
All rights reserved.

It is illegal to copy, distribute, or create derivative works from this book in whole or in part or to contribute to the copying, distribution, or creating of derivative works of this book.

No portion of this book may be reproduced, stored in a retrieval system, or transmitted in any form or by any means—electronic, mechanical, photocopying, recording or otherwise—without written permission from the publisher.

Photographs, illustrations, cover design, and literary content by mOjAf.
Book design and layout by Timeless Treasures Publishing.

Published by Timeless Treasures Publishing
P.O. Box 278
Crossnore, NC 28616
www.TimelessTreasuresStudio.net
info@TimelessTreasuresStudio.net

First edition: June, 2023.

Paperback ISBN: 978-1-953940-40-7
Hardcover ISBN: 978-1-953940-41-4
E-Book ISBN: 978-1-953940-42-1

Manufactured in the United States of America.

Disclaimer: This book details the author's personal experiences with and opinions about synchronicity, personal happiness, and other topics. This book is not intended to be used to treat any medical or emotional condition. For those issues, please consult a licensed healthcare practitioner.

This book is dedicated to my amazing cousin, JONATHAN. Thank you for being my forever Angel, friend, companion, teacher, inspiration, and little brother. Thank you, also, for being the example for how to live with kindness, compassion, love, and a childlike wonder and enthusiasm every day, and continuously showing me how to treat everyone like they are the most important thing in the moment.

You are the most SPECIAL person in my life. I love you beyond words and will always cherish our moments together.

I want to give a sincere thank you to the little team of people who have helped me to live my lifelong dream of becoming a writer.

This book has come to fruition thanks to the tireless work, care and insight from Danica De La Mora and her amazing mother, Nancy Stroupe. Thank you so much for your patience and understanding of my journey.

I want to thank Angelo for all that he has done for me and for being my own personal "shark," which has allowed this dream to be fulfilled. Thank you, my brother!

HINTS 4 HAPPINESS
CONTENTS

Introduction: Three Missions 1

Breaking the Pencil (BTP) 3

Try Letting the Day Happen to You 4-6

Be Here Now 7-12

Smelling the Roses 12-14

Being on Purpose 14-17

Try Being Grateful For Everything 17-19

Having No Regrets 20

Ask For Forgiveness 21-22

Try Getting Comfortable with Death 22-30

Try Not to Whine or Complain 30-32

Don't Complain, Don't Criticize, Don't Condemn 32-33

Try Being A Peaceful Warrior 33-36

P.O.M. - Peace of mind 37-38

Try Not Sweating the Small Stuff 38-40
Try Laughing Out Loud and Often 40-41
Try Spreading Only Joy 42-44
Clock Stoppers 44-46
Try to Be Like Mathieu 46-48
A Few of My Favorite Compliments 48-49
Enjoy the Day 49-51
Dealing with Physical Pain and Discomfort 51-53
Whatever You Focus Your Mind on Expands 53-54
Creating the Perfect Day 54-56
Waking Up Spiritually 56-60
Try Reconnecting with Your Inner Child 60-62
Try Living Like You're Dying 62-63
Try Singing Out Loud 63-64
Try to Not Worry What Others Think 65-69
Try to Minimize or Even Eliminate Worrying 69-70
Try Watching and Listening to Happy Things 71-72
Anything Except Politics or Religion 73

Try Hanging Out with the HAPPY 74-75

Just Be.... HAPPY 76-78

Try Finding a BALANCE In All Areas 79-81

Try the JOE WALSH RULE 81-84

Try Being Nice Like the 3 B's 84-86

Try Following the GOLDEN RULE 86-88

Try Serving Others 88-89

Try Being a Mensch 90-91

Try Making EVERYONE Feel SPECIAL 91-93

Try NOT Hurting ANYONE'S feelings 93-95

The City Can Make You Mean 95-96

Try to Not Judge ANYONE 96-97

Include EVERYONE 98-99

Try to Be Less Dependent on Others 99-100

Getting Butt Hurt 101

Let It Be 102-103

Try Learning Every Day 103-104

Try Taking Care of Yourself First 105-106

Try Not Being a Burden to ANYONE 106-108

Blame Only Causes Pain 108-109

List That Help Us Grow and Learn 109-112

Treat All Beings with Respect 112-113

Appreciating Nature 113-114

Childlike Wonder 115-118

Ask the Universe for Help or What You Need 118-119

Understanding That We're All CONNECTED 120-121

We Are All In This Together 122-124

Finding JOY In the JOY of Others, Even Strangers 124-125

Feeding Ducks, Squirrels Et Al 126

FRIENDSHIP 126-132

Introduce Others 132-134

Try Believing in EARTH ANGELS 134-136

The Music of Our Lives 137-140

FINDING, EXPERIENCING & LIVING IN HAPPINESS 140-146

HINTS 4 HAPPINESS

 **INTRODUCTION**

This book is a description of how I found joy after so many years of living without pure happiness. My hope is that it will act as a manual for achieving such happiness for anyone who truly wants to live each day with an extreme level of PEACE, JOY, FUN, ADVENTURE, LOVE AND **HAPPINESS!**

People who knew me before my spiritual transformation may not have thought I was fully miserable, but certainly those close to me were acutely aware of my many frustrations with life. I was fortunate enough still to have some really good friends, even though I could often be extremely impatient, cocky, rude, entitled, obnoxious and judgmental. Only a few people saw through that abrasive exterior that I spent so much of my life creating. I had built the proverbial "brick wall" around the kind, compassionate, loving soul that became encased inside.

One of my earliest friends described the change after I told him of my recently-found peace. He said, "Before, I knew you had moments of joy, but I never heard you sound this joyous." He was exactly right. I did have moments of happiness throughout the years, though now I would call them times of pleasure.

The DIFFERENCE, I realized through my studies, is that there had to be a reason for those moments of pleasure, like being on vacation or in the perfect setting for a good time. Those times are very easy to enjoy. Now I have peaceful joy and contentment throughout my everyday life. These moments happen at home alone, while walking through my town or

HINTS 4 HAPPINESS

anywhere, and even at work, which before was completely unfathomable! I will do my best to explain how these changes occurred with a sincere hope that others can find the same remarkable result. Upon thorough self-examination of this spiritual growth process, I have discovered and will describe the three missions that I have chosen to live by for the remainder of my time here on Earth that have led to and contribute to my daily **HAPPINESS:**

I. TO WAKE UP FEELING GRATEFUL FOR EACH NEW DAY, THEN TO LIVE FULLY WITH JOY, PEACE, FUN, SPONTANEITY, AND A CHILDLIKE WONDER, BEING PRESENT THROUGHOUT.

II. TO BE A GOOD PERSON, STRIVE TO BE EVEN BETTER AND TO CONTINUE TO GROW SPIRITUALLY.

III. TO CONNECT WITH THE UNIVERSE AND LEAVE IT BETTER FOR HAVING BEEN HERE.

I believe my true peace and HAPPINESS came to me when I started to live these missions. Since the time of my AWAKENING, I have been compiling and documenting the changes I made to achieve this contentment. I believe anyone can greatly increase his or her HAPPINESS by following the heart of these guidelines. Everyone has his or her own specific mission that will ultimately lead to contentment, so I encourage you, as many have coached me, to define your own missions or guidelines to keep you in your PATH TO HAPPINESS! Make the CHOICE TO BE HAPPY and enjoy the full experience of the day.

LIVING WITH JOY, PEACE, AND HAPPINESS

 BREAKING THE PENCIL

In the movie *Groundhog Day,* which has so many life lessons throughout, Bill Murray's character, Phil Connor, quickly becomes frustrated with his stagnant situation. He is stuck reliving the same day. So, before he goes to bed, he breaks the pencil from behind his ear to see if tomorrow hopefully will be different. I have taken this scene as my own personal philosophy to make sure that there is enough variety, spontaneity and excitement in life. Breaking the pencil, which I sometimes abbreviate as BTP, means to say "yes" when you often would say "no." Stop saying no to the friendly neighbor who keeps inviting you over. Stay out a little later on a school night. Say yes to a last-minute trip, though you feel too exhausted to go. You most likely will be happy you did, especially if you attack it like Phil did at the end of the movie.

This discussion also brings up a point I discovered a few years back. My good friend Frank and I were discussing movies, just after talking about self-improvement and philosophy. He said to me, "Well, movies don't change your life." I didn't respond at that moment, but upon further reflection, I told him that I disagreed. In *Groundhog Day*, Phil starts out as an egotistical, obnoxious, narcissist with little or no compassion. At the end of the movie, he is the complete opposite. Many people feel this movie is religious in a way because of Phil's triumphant transformation. I agree. I have personally used Phil's example at times to keep my cool and show equanimity like Phil at the end of the movie rather than react obnoxiously like Phil at the beginning. Looking back now, I can see that I have actually made the same dramatic

HINTS 4 HAPPINESS

changes that Phil did. I also do believe that movies like this one and others like *The Shack*, which I'll dive into later, have absolutely aided in my awakening.

Like many other philosophies, techniques or secrets to **JOY** that I have learned from others or discovered along the way, I shared BTP with my good friends. Now when they do something fun, spontaneous, or outrageous, they will tell me that they are **BREAKING THE PENCIL.**

My mission is accomplished when I help others experience more fun, joy and adventure in their lives. Ultimately, I know this discovery will lead to greater **HAPPINESS** for them. The knowledge that I have aided in their **happiness** then, in fact, greatly **INCREASES MY OWN HAPPINESS!!!**

This situation is a **Win-Win** one. **If everyone focused on only Win-Win outcomes, IMAGINE what our world would be like!**

 TRY LETTING THE DAY HAPPEN TO YOU

I think I first heard this phrase from a bar customer/ friend for whom I have tremendous respect. He is an ex-military guy who battled for our country in the Middle East. My understanding is he was one of the bad asses who was involved in a situation similar to the one portrayed in the movie *Black Hawk Down*. When I met him out in public at a restaurant or bar, he was soft spoken, calm, and almost seemed indifferent to his surroundings. I could, however, sense that he was acutely aware of everything around him. We were making small talk when he mentioned that, as a philosophy,

LIVING WITH JOY, PEACE, AND HAPPINESS

he liked to "not worry about the day, but instead let the day worry about him." I'm not sure if he actually allows this concept to happen often or if he just strives for such a goal, but I loved the concept immediately.

I was brought up in a very business-oriented atmosphere where thoughtful planning was common and often required. I spent my life setting goals and stressing over fighting for and accomplishing those achievements. This kind of self-pressure created tremendous amounts of discomfort over the years. Whether the goal was financial, status-driven, or even romantic in nature, the fear of failure and the desire to succeed could cause heartbreaking disappointment when not realized. This newfound philosophy has had a tremendous impact on my peace of mind.

A night comes to mind when I was invited to a casual dinner party/grill-out with a couple with whom I was friendly. We had discussed getting together several times. This night, I didn't come up with some reason not to attend.

There were a few other mutual acquaintances there, one being an attractive young blonde, whom I often compared to the lovely actress Kate Hudson (daughter of Goldie Hawn). When I saw her in attendance and unencumbered, I couldn't help but wonder, "What if?" Why couldn't something romantic or sexual happen between this 22-ish girl and me, a 45-ish old guy? I started just to appreciate the wonderful setting for this evening, that followed on the heels of a peaceful, fun afternoon off. We were at their cool little apartment, when my buddy's recent words came

HINTS 4 HAPPINESS

to mind. Rather than running out on the back deck to catch up with this cute girl and the other guests who had gone out to smoke, I remained in the apartment just to "take in" the beauty of the day and the current atmosphere. I gave up all attachment to the outcome with this girl. I actually seemed to be more needed by this other guy, a Georgia fan rival of mine, as I am a proud Gator myself. He was in the middle of an ongoing break up with his wife. I bonded with him and the hosting couple in a way that I knew would be significant moving forward, and I couldn't help but note that this outcome was more important than trying "to land" this college girl. Letting go of a somewhat unrealistic goal and just being in the moment was simply beautiful.

Jay Shetty is a former monk and now is an author and spiritual teacher. In his book, THINK LIKE A MONK, which I highly recommend, he says to try to go somewhere new about once a month. I love this concept and I even try to accomplish this goal more like one a week. We can be creatures of habit and, if we take it too far, it can prevent us from experiencing new things. Even if it's something as simple and small as exploring a new street in my neighborhood, there is a certain feeling I get when I'm discovering a new spot. Some of us have an adventurous spirit, which I understand is only about one out of five people. We are the ones who LOVE TO BREAK THE FRIGGIN' PENCIL! If it's something really momentous, novel, and different from our norm, I like to say I SHATTERED THE PENCIL!!!

That's why you'll also NEVER hear me give that dreaded response I hear from unconscious people when you ask how they are. Some say "Same

LIVING WITH JOY, PEACE, AND HAPPINESS

◆ **BE HERE NOW**

old, same old." I don't say that, because I strive to keep a good balance of variety in my day and that keeps it always interesting.

This saying has many meanings to me now. I go over certain guidelines for each day. You might call them reminders and the number two goal each day is to **Be Here Now!!** Crows cawing, flowers blooming, and the sun rising are events that I have pretty much ignored for the last forty years of my life. Now, for whatever reason, I am aware of such happenings and I'm often quite fascinated with these natural occurrences. I actually seek them out to revel in their wonder. The observance of these natural beauties seems to energize me and nourish my very being. They now feel magical.

One of my favorite things to do is hang out in bars. My father was a functional alcoholic, which seems to be fairly common in restaurant families. I was born into the New York Stampler family, who were well-known restauranteurs in Manhattan back in the '50s, '60s and '70s, if not sooner. My father was the fifth-straight-generation restaurant owner. I would be the sixth, if I ever fully took the plunge and owned one. I remember hearing my grandparents boasting about how their Stefan, my beloved father, was bellied up to the bar drinking Scotch at about four years old. His love of Scotch and bars stayed with him until his death and, though I'm not a Scotch drinker, I do drink a bit and I love the feel at an old school dive bar. I feel I get more enjoyment out of the social experience than the drinking itself, but maybe that's a rationalization to protect myself from the fear of duplicating my

HINTS 4 HAPPINESS

father's behavior.

Either way, let's just say I like the bars. It is one of my favorite hobbies and, though I've tried for years to replace it with other, healthier hobbies, I believe it will always be a part of my life, and I'm good with that. I think many of us "bar flies" feel this ritual refreshes us or re-energizes us to go forward to the next day of work. This feeling is especially true for those of us who remain single, although I think in many cases married folks enjoy this little escape from their other half as well. What I have discovered over the last year or so is that I can gain as much refreshment, nourishment, and peace from my morning activities as the bar experience. This discovery is fairly spectacular to me. As I write this morning at 9:00 a.m. before my bartender job, I am feeling at 10 on a HAPPINESS scale of 1 to 10. I could not have dreamed of this phenomenon just a year ago and it is what I mean by being here now!

Another major meaning for me regarding the saying "Be Here Now" is, of course, the amazing book by one of my most significant spiritual teachers, the late, great Ram Dass. His book was handed to me a couple of years ago by a good friend whose nickname is Redneck Hippy Jesus. He informed me that some pages might connect deeply with me, while some might not and that statement was very accurate for me. Ram's story bonded me to him immediately because we have had a similar journey in our very business-oriented, Northern,

LIVING WITH JOY, PEACE, AND HAPPINESS

Jewish upbringing. We were both thoroughly compelled by our families to strive to achieve financial and academic success with little focus on our actual psychological happiness. We both got caught up in making a future, rather than living in the present. Ram Dass, having achieved much of the American Dream as a respected psychologist and exalted Harvard professor, eventually realized that his path was not the proper one to pure inner joy. I, too, found this to be true as I climbed the ladder of success. I like to say I climbed halfway up that ladder, didn't appreciate the view or the people there, said "F this," and slid back down said ladder. I ended up gliding like a fireman, down the pole into pure joy, peace, and happiness.

Also impacting me profoundly while I was reading Ram's *Be Here Now,* was the section on the stages of **chakra**. I had been introduced to the concept of chakras when I was seeing a psychotherapist several years ago. I didn't quite understand the techniques the therapist used back then or his explanation of them in general, but the way Ram Dass wrote about the journey of growth made complete sense to me at the perfect time for me to accept it. My belief is that I had already pursued the first three stages and was firmly in the fourth.

The first stage (of survival) is one we still struggle with from conception. Eventually most survival techniques become second nature. Secondly, we strive for sexual or romantic needs. The third stage becomes a focus on the financial or other forms of success to which we are "trained" to aspire. I believe the second and third phase can happen in either order. I knew upon reading *Be Here Now* that I had already been through the first three sections of desires. I was changing dramatically at the time and I knew that those first three stages were no longer my focus. Then I read the phrase

HINTS 4 HAPPINESS

"Compassionate Oneness" in stage four. This stage spoke of a certain awareness that negative feelings towards others accomplish nothing and, in fact, only hurt us.

In my case, there was a realization and an awakening happening that showed me we are really all in it together. There was a profound loss of any resentment of anyone. It was almost as if I had exhausted myself with all of those pessimistic and negative emotions during my previous fifty or so years alive. I didn't want to be that guy anymore. I recognized easily that I was to that point and it felt amazing. I finally had some clear sign that I was, in fact, growing and improving. I felt joy, happiness, and peace that were difficult to properly describe. It was gorgeous. I remember communicating my joyous discovery to a couple of my confidants and explaining how I would love to remain in this wonderful "happy place" for a while. I wanted to marinate in this beautiful feeling of personal growth and satisfactory accomplishment. There were hints that I couldn't remain there long; I was going to have to keep moving forward in the book and in life.

When I looked ahead in the *Be Here Now* book, the next stage referred to God and religion. In the last couple of years, I had made the discovery that I had slowly changed from a non-believer in God to an agnostic. When I read the part about God, I felt that it was not important right now. I decided to skip this section, since I felt I had already made that change to agnosticism recently enough that I didn't need to push this aspect right now. I looked ahead to the next chakra stage, which turned out to be knowledge and wisdom. Perfect, I thought. I am thirsting for knowledge at an accelerated rate. But then God presented himself to me in many magical ways, showing me that this journey of growth is leading me and I

LIVING WITH JOY, PEACE, AND HAPPINESS

must follow along.

Before this time, as mentioned, especially while I was growing up, I had no real belief that there was, in fact, a GOD. I grew up Jewish (you might say barely practicing the religion) and my parents did their best to teach us children the wonderful traditions of Judaism. We were considered about the least religious of the sects of Jews, known as "reformed" or "liberal" compared to the very religious orthodox or Hasidic Jews. Those groups, who are much more conservative types, keep kosher homes and have much stricter rules and traditions that are kept weekly or even daily. My upbringing was much more relaxed, like others in my family's social circle. We celebrated only the high holy days of Yom Kippur and the commercial big holidays like Chanukah and Passover. I did have a Bar Mitzvah, a "coming of age" for any Jewish person, which was a wonderful experience. However, all through the many religious holidays, events and other times in the Temple, I just didn't believe there was a God. My parents rarely, if ever, spoke of God. I'm not blaming them, by any means. That just wasn't our upbringing. We were NOT religious.

Now, let me go back to that time in life when I was connecting with Ram Dass's *Be Here Now*, and the book was stating that the next stage of life for me was GOD. I really tried to say, **"No, I'm good."** But God said, **"YES!"**

Many small **miracles** started to becoming apparent in my life and these events will be discussed throughout these pages from the magical white crow, to the walk in Key Largo, to the cosmic Joke in Boca, to my second wind. I received clear "messages" from the Universe and God that were resounding *confirmations* that He is there, watching, rooting and LOVING US!

 SMELLING THE ROSES

This old cliché has had renewed meaning for me over the last year and a half, or so. I mentioned briefly about flowers blooming and as of this April morning, while spring is fully upon us in the midst of the coronavirus epidemic, the adage feels like an appropriate motto. During my mindful walks, I often stop along the way to actually sniff the flowers to enhance the peaceful, beautiful and grateful feelings towards the Universe. Any form of nature seems to do so for us. I believe this action stimulates our body and mind in a profound way and truly can bring us into the moment. The larger the natural form, the greater the effect appears to be, although the intensity with which we feel this energy depends on us. When I take my walks to my beloved neighborhood mill pond to feed the ducks and geese or to take in the wonderful waterfall, my connection with nature energizes me and confirms that everything is good in the world. Smelling the roses.

of course, is also a great metaphor for not taking the present for granted and not rushing through to the next task.

Many great authors and texts have discussed keeping your eyes on the prize or the goal. These types of motivational sayings were inspiring to me at certain times in life when I was material or outcome goal-focused. They can be useful in keeping one attached to the pot of gold at the end of the rainbow. Now, after fifty years of living, I recognize that the struggles to reach certain goals, even those ultimately unachieved, were some of the best parts of the journey. Also, the amazing little things that happened along the way often eclipsed the goal itself upon reflection. For example, in my early years during and after college, I packed my whole car up and moved across the country to Los Angeles three different times. On all of these occasions, I had all of my belongings with me and barely had any real destination in mind. One could surmise that none of those relocations led to a successful outcome. I left California each time without realizing my dream of making it big in Hollywood.

As I look back or discuss these experiences in detail, it is obvious that so many of them were special, even magical, moments in my life. I got to attend events like the Emmy Awards, a Woody Allen movie premiere, went skydiving and skiing in amazing places and rubbed elbows with the likes of Arnold Schwarzenegger, Magic Johnson and some of the most beautiful models in the world. Even with all these exciting happenings, if you had asked me back then if I felt successful or fulfilled, the answer would have been, no friggin' way, because I was too focused on the outcome. People often say, "Those were the good old days." I like the updated, more conscious version, "These *are* the good old days."

HINTS 4 HAPPINESS

Movies like *Forrest Gump* can teach us and sometimes remind us of such lessons in life. The way Forrest knew to pay attention to sunsets and other beautiful scenery along his journey was telling us to do the same. No matter what seemed to be happening in his life, he still seemed to appreciate and take note of these quiet, peaceful moments in life with NATURE. I aspire to do the same throughout each day. Once you start to notice these simple pleasures, it becomes easier and easier to see these miracles. There is beauty even in the swamp, if only we look.

 BEING ON PURPOSE

It has taken me between thirty-two and fifty years to truly figure out my true self and what I am meant to do during my time on this planet. I am now over fifty years of age and my path and journey are finally clear. My recollection of starting on this quest for self-improvement and self-realization goes back to my first year in college. I believe that this odyssey most likely began at birth or even before, but the increased desire for psychological knowledge and self-examination became prominent after I finished high school. It was about that time when I began to look at myself and realize that I didn't like many things about the personality that I had adopted as my own. Back then I didn't know that the shell I had developed was not really

LIVING WITH JOY, PEACE, AND HAPPINESS

me. I did, however, realize at about age eighteen that I didn't want to be so negative, so mean and, at least superficially, so callous. It took my witnessing someone up close who was so pessimistic and whiny for me to realize how unpleasant she was to be around. Then it dawned on me that other people most likely felt the same way about me. This realization added a new mission to my life at that time. I was trying to figure out why I was miserable in my first year at the University of Florida at the same time I was trying to chase that American Dream to keep my parents proud. Also, I knew I had to try to fix my sour personality.

Others have voiced a few different ways regarding our search for meaning and purpose in our lives as well as discovering or reconnecting with our true inner selves. It is easier to look at what we don't want in life or who we don't want to represent as ourselves and then eliminate those qualities from our existence. This examination and work on ourselves can then reshape our personality and our lifestyle to create a life on purpose with more peace, joy and contentment and far less stress, worry and suffering. This philosophy has worked magically for me to fine-tune my life. I examined and studied thoroughly the factors that created more peace and then I followed that blueprint to form the simple, peaceful, joyous life I am now living fully.

I am now fully aware that my purpose, having figured out the key to my own **HAPPINESS, is to help others** find theirs. This process first involves showing people how to find out what they truly want in life and then guiding them toward that achievement. I believe that happiness is the goal for most of us, although many people don't even know what will make them happy. Just like I was in my past, people are distracted by physical desires because society impresses upon us that these material items will equal contentment. This outcome is rarely the case. If there is joy or happiness connected with the realization of external desires, this elation is usually short-lived. True happiness comes from within and is otherwise achieved from living by noble principles and fulfilling positive emotions that enhance our connection with others and the universe.

As I have mentioned, it is easiest to find out what we want or what will make us happy by first understanding what makes us unhappy or unfulfilled. The thoughts that cause us stress and make us feel bad about ourselves are often caused by regret for how we behave towards others in certain circumstances. Once I realized that following the principles of kindness and the **GOLDEN RULE,** even when life is chaotic and it seems impossible to do so, eliminates feelings of regret afterwards. With this understanding and clarity, it becomes easier to stay calm and nice in any circumstance. It then gets so easy with continuous practice that it becomes natural or **NORMAL.**

(Sunday 3/28/21 Passover)
Drank about 1/16 of liquid mushrooms. It's been a rainy 50-degree spring morning that may be gloomy to some but is wonderfully ominous to my kind. As the rain lifted, the puffy white clouds lovingly blanketed our cozy mountain town. I had a comfortable, blue-lit shower where I had some warm "shroomy" epiphanies. I put off the only slight concern I face in life, which is how to make a few more bucks to pay my bills without infringing on the amazing, peaceful bliss I glide in daily. The free time is crucial for me to continue on this equanimous path as I rationalize maybe a little that these three days off I currently enjoy allow me to properly contemplate

LIVING WITH JOY, PEACE, AND HAPPINESS

what to do with my life when I truly GROW UP! It slowly becomes apparent that I am already DOING IT!

 TRY BEING GRATEFUL FOR EVERYTHING

The longer I live, the more objective I seem to have gotten about everything. I can now look back at and evaluate certain behaviors that I have exhibited in my fifty-plus years, usually through observing similar actions by others around me. Insights also have become apparent by witnessing or hearing of the lives that others have experienced. Many, many people all over the world and even here have had to endure far more difficulties than I have. My upper-middle-class upbringing in suburban New Jersey was loaded with pool parties, circus trips, fine restaurants and – most importantly –

HINTS 4 HAPPINESS

much love and affection, mostly from my adoring mother and maternal grandparents. My struggles along the way mainly consisted of my own internal conflicts caused by my own insecurity, fear, and search for meaning. I never lacked for food or shelter. I am not a big fan of watching the news because I find it incredibly negative and sad. I do try to watch just a half hour each day just to be kept in the loop of the world's happenings. The upside to viewing such is that it does highlight the great struggles that others have lived through and continue to deal with in many places. If we keep the proper perspective and realize that others have had far worse challenges than we have, then we should have no problem facing our meager troubles with a positive attitude. One of the most important things is to remember how lucky we are, regardless of how bad each particular day seems to be going.

LIVING WITH JOY, PEACE, AND HAPPINESS

At this point, the level of awareness that we have becomes a factor. Consciousness is another word used to describe this phenomenon. How can a rational human being watch a news story of an Ethiopian child who is literally starving to death, homeless, and disease-ridden and then shut off the television, only to then complain that their expensive steak was slightly overcooked? I definitely was one of those people. I am as embarrassed of my behavior then as I am proud that I now realize how unaware I was. I am so grateful for everything. I can now finish a day, like I did today, and be so grateful for the simplicity of mainly lying in bed, and then connecting with a very special few. The cherry on the day was a frozen dinner, done extremely well by Michael Angelo's. As I was eating this bachelor-style meal, it struck me how thoroughly and incredibly pleased I was with it. It was then followed by a bowl of butter pecan ice cream with raisins and chocolate syrup. It was GLORIOUS! I guess it just makes me kind of proud to know that I can be so grateful and it takes very little to let me feel spoiled. I don't need fancy restaurants or expensive takeout. If I'm not cooking myself, I can just have something like Michael Angelo's (Frozen) Baked Ziti and I'm in heaven. Of course, I am usually there anyway – right in that 9.5 to 10-plus range on the SCALE OF HAPPINESS. Let's call it the Magic Zone.

MAGIC ZONE – That's where I live

I never want to complain about anything. I'm not perfect in this regard. I don't know that anyone can be. I know that I'm far better than I was and I will continue to strive to do better. Like PROVERBS says, "Don't complain, don't criticize, don't condemn." I GUARANTEE this advice will make you happier in the long run of life.

HAVING NO REGRETS

One of the feelings or emotions that seem to cause us so much pain is regret. When my mind used to wander later in the day or even sometimes in the morning, it often would seem to settle on things about which I feel sorry or guilty. It can be something as simple and insignificant as having made a remark that may or may not have been taken the wrong way by a coworker to a situation far deeper, such as choosing not to attend a family member's funeral. The latter example could linger in one's mind for a lifetime where the former should pass in minutes, hours, or – worst case – by the end of the week. The truth is that it can depend on how well we control our thoughts. But it also will always revert back to whether you handled the experience properly. Specifically, your intentions at the time will matter with respect given to the capabilities you possessed at that time in your journey.

I have found that if you are living righteously and on purpose, you are more prepared to take the best action during those challenging times to have no reason to judge yourself in the future. Or, at least if you look back, you are comfortable with the fact that you tried to do the right thing but weren't "equipped" to handle it any better. You then gather extra peace in knowing that you are now fully capable of doing an even better job the next time similar predicaments arise. These acknowledgments lead to being happier on a daily basis. In the case of the possibly offensive comment at work, I now believe that I am more careful with such casual speech so as to be less likely to hurt someone's feelings in the future. This awareness also adds to my feelings of contentment each day.

LIVING WITH JOY, PEACE, AND HAPPINESS

 ASK FOR FORGIVENESS

Another way to understand and not be weighed down by regret is to ask forgiveness. Knowing that none of us is perfect should allow us to forgive ourselves when we make mistakes. When we do act in a way that we realize is not congruent with our values or beliefs, the best way to prevent or cease feelings of dismay is to go to the source of the pain and make it right. Many times, we are feeling bad because of things we said, as mentioned, or we didn't show proper empathy for others when needed. If there is someone we can go to in order to make things right, that is usually the best choice.

Learning to apologize is one of the most important lessons that I was fortunate enough to learn fairly early in life. I've heard the question asked, "Would you rather be peaceful or right?" and I believe having true piece of mind comes with understanding that we don't always have to be right. Who is right all the time? **NOBODY!** Well, maybe God is! So, when we are aware enough to recognize when we are wrong, the best thing we can do is to apologize and humbly ask for forgiveness. Have you ever met some of those stubborn people who NEVER admit when they are wrong? These people are so attached to EGO that they don't have any idea what honesty is. They are living BLINDLY!!! Some will flat out say they will never apologize. These are people I tend to avoid. What they are saying basically is that they are never wrong, and we already covered the fact that NOBODY is flawless.

If there is no way to apologize for my indiscretion, then I make a sincere

HINTS 4 HAPPINESS

commitment to myself to never repeat the mistake.

 TRY GETTING COMFORTABLE WITH DEATH

Dealing with death felt like a natural next topic after regret. This is because for many the hardest part of dealing with someone's passing is that we may feel we didn't appreciate, spend more time with, love enough or even didn't bond with or forgive that person more easily. In some cases, maybe we even had an open wound with that person and there was no closure to that gap when death occurred.

I experienced just this situation with my bar customer and friend James. He was a weathered sixty-ish guy who used to own a bar in a neighboring small town. I believe he had some family money, but he wasn't one to brag or flaunt it. For the couple years I knew him, he'd come in for two or three beers, we'd shoot the shit about life or sports, and he'd be gone before dark. He was slightly cranky occasionally, but he was mostly patient, upbeat, and friendly. On our last day together, he asked me to change the Yankee baseball game that I had on a couple of the televisions. He, being a southern gentleman, and me, being New York born, it was probably partly a

friendly civil war-type jab. Since I was characteristically moody myself in those days, I jabbed right back with something over the top like, "How 'bout I put your game on every TV in the house? Would that make you happy, James?" We went to our separate corners and, after a while, I noticed he had left. He didn't give me his normal salutation so I wondered if he were mad enough to not tip me, but his usual generous gratuity was there.

About a week later, the aforementioned regret collided with that death thing as I started to hear rumors that our friend James may have passed away. I felt the proverbial punch-in-the-gut feeling for most of the day as our fears were realized. He was gone. How could I ever feel at peace with James when I was rude to him in our last encounter on Earth?

I struggled with this concern up until the day of the funeral. Around this time, in the last few years, I was starting to catch on to totally controlling my thoughts. I knew how lousy I was feeling in light of my last experience with James, but I was also well aware that there was nothing I could do to change it. My goal on the day of the funeral was to be there with my buddies to mourn our lost pal and keep it as beautiful and positive as possible. It turned out to be a gorgeous, sunny, clear day in the NC mountains as we gathered to say our farewells. When I saw James's coffin, I walked by him and said my apologies. I felt a certain comfort as I teared up, hoping that he understood how much I cared for him and would miss his presence at work.

After the ceremony, I went for lunch and a couple drinks with some other customers and a work buddy at an Italian joint on the way home. I was in

HINTS 4 HAPPINESS

full realization that this was the first time I was hanging with some of these guys outside of the bar. I knew this would bind us from then on. One of the regulars who was becoming like family gave me a gift at that restaurant that I will cherish forever. Gary is a seventy-something Vietnam vet who sometimes seems like the mascot of the bar. He's lovable, loud and just plain homey. He is the kind of guy you worry about if he doesn't show up to drink a few days in a row. He was as close to James as anyone in our little crew that day. I was concerned about him most as was my good buddy Burton, because Gary had some health issues and he was the oldest of those of us who went to the service.

So, Gary says at lunch, almost with a Forrest Gump smirk, "James told me you had words that day." I was all ears, of course, to hear what he was going to say next. He continued, "He was ill about it." I was then, and still am, learning the mountain slang up here and I wasn't sure what he meant.

"You mean he was mad at me?" I blurted.

"No," he said, "he wasn't mad. He said you had words over the damn TVs." Gary then said something else to confirm that James had indeed enjoyed our times together. I felt a huge weight of guilt soar off my shoulders and I stepped outside to grasp the gravity of that moment. Again, I teared up and spoke to James.

I learned several things from that funeral. One was to choose my words and reactions to people more wisely, because you never know when that will be the last thing you say to them. A second was that if I have ever had an opportunity to give someone a priceless gift with words like Gary did for me, then I should jump on it. Yet another lesson was that a sad day at a funeral can also be quite moving, beautiful and momentous if we only choose the proper perspective.

As a child, I was extremely fearful of dying. I can remember several occasions of crying at bedtime or other times because of my concerns about the end of life. Usually, my mother tried to comfort me in those times, but as affectionate, caring, and loving as she was, there never seemed to be anything she could say to get me past this worry. I can remember clearly my thoughts about death that I would reiterate over the years during these breakdowns. I would explain to my mother, "I know that I won't die for a very long time, but then what?"

I'm sure she did bring up Heaven or something to calm me, but I just wasn't buying it. The end, no matter how far away in time it seemed, was downright terrifying to me, enough that it kept me up many nights and certainly caused my mother stress and pain in dealing with those fears of mine. Back then, as a child and for most of my life, I didn't believe in God. I guess this made it difficult to have faith in any kind of Heaven or afterlife. Now, finally after all those years of worrying about the inevitable cessation of life, I am at total ease with the future.

Ram Dass described how his teacher, Majaraji, spoke of dying, **DEATH IS LIKE TAKING OFF A TIGHT SHOE.** I now truly believe that this is how it will be for me.

As of today, 12-14-22, I am dealing with death up close and personal. My landlord and dear friend died. He also happened to be one of the most

HINTS 4 HAPPINESS

honorable and beloved members of our little mountain town. Judge Alec had a long, extensive career in community and public service. He taught at both Appalachian State University and Lees-McRae College in the North Carolina High Country. Then he went on to become a local lawyer and, ultimately, a judge in Avery County, where he became widely known and respected as a fair and caring judge. He died yesterday after a bout with dementia, which left him virtually speechless for the last couple of years.

I had met the Judge and his wife a couple of years ago at a company party for the Italian Restaurant where I tend bar. His wife, Brenda, who also happens to be the mayor of our awesome, quaint little mountain town, and the Judge were sitting nearby when I was introduced to them. The Mayor informed me that the Judge couldn't hear very well, which of course was true, but also it was a way of quietly explaining his lack of talkativeness. For me, his verbal communication was never really necessary. His eyes immediately caught mine and that connection was followed by the most genuine and sweet, almost childlike smile. I was hooked instantly.

We were all drinking and enjoying the festivities, so I decided I'd like to have a shot with the Judge. When I suggested it, the Mayor quickly cautioned that he had had enough to drink already. Now, I'll admit this is a little pet peeve of mine when spouses decide how much or what their partner can or can't do! I feel we and only we ourselves should be allowed to make such decisions. Of course, as is often the case, I was proven wrong here, as the Judge later was reluctant to walk down the stairs when it was time to leave the party. There is not much question that my shots with the Judge caused some or all of his issues that night. It was completely my fault. I felt bad, of course.

LIVING WITH JOY, PEACE, AND HAPPINESS

For the next year or two, I saw the couple out and about from time to time. Often, I would also see the Judge sitting on the porch in front of the most lovely, homey, *Mayberry*-esque, *Happy Days*-like house in the center or our little downtown.

I was starting to feel God's presence more and more and had increased my meditations. I was coming through the process of my "SPIRITUAL AWAKENING." I was beginning to understand how to MANIFEST things.

So, eventually, when many of my fellow restaurant workers were getting booted from their apartments because of the rising costs of housing in an area with no available rentals, I found myself in the same situation. My rental apartment was about to be sold and, though I was originally promised an option to buy, I was now told that I had about three weeks to MOVE OUT! I was fairly upset at first, but then I just decided to ACCEPT the FLOW of LIFE and meditate on what I should do next.

I had been given insight by at least two or three sources (making it yet another Universal Confirmation) that the period early in the morning was the best time to "receive" such answers from the UNIVERSE. Hindu Yogi Sadghuru says that 3:40 a.m. is the opportune time to HEAR such MESSAGES. Another source from my reading said, "The morning mist has answers; don't go back to sleep."

So, the next early morning when I "happened" to be thoroughly awake at just that perfect time, I went into a deep, calm, meditative state and asked the UNIVERSE for the answer to my little apartment dilemma. After falling back asleep, I awoke at my usual 7:00 a.m. The answer came to me

HINTS 4 HAPPINESS

clearly. It said, "talk to the Mayor." I knew that was my direction, but I had no clue how soon it would happen.

I got in my car to head to work and, at the bottom of my street where the stop sign was, there was the Mayor, walking her two dogs! I was starting to get used to these kinds of SYNCHRONICITIES, so it wasn't that shocking to see her, but the way it continues is to me, in every way, MIRACULOUS.

So, I got out of my car and said hello to the Mayor and her dogs. After trading pleasantries, I brought up the fact that many of my restaurant pals were going through this housing problem and we discussed the overall housing shortage for us middle-classers. As usual, she was understanding and sympathetic of what my friends and others were going through. Then I mentioned that I, too, was now looking for a place and she right away spoke of how she had just shown her rental place to someone. She lamented that she had already shown him, but she said it might be too small for his needs.

I was in a three bedroom at the time. I knew I didn't need that much space. In fact, in another UNIVERSAL CONFIRMATION and/or MANIFESTATION, I recall thinking how I would be fine with a one bedroom with a loft for needy friends who could use a crashing spot. So, the Mayor said that the gentleman who looked at the place was going to let her know by Monday. I asked the Mayor if I could give her my number, just in case the guy decided

LIVING WITH JOY, PEACE, AND HAPPINESS

to pass on the place. She liked that idea, too, and she took my number. I went on to work and hoped for the best.

Then, in the next day or two, I meditated once more on the fact that I would be fine if I had to leave town even like others, but that I really would prefer to stay right downtown if the UNIVERSE and GOD were good with that. I actually prayed in the hope that this man would decide that the tiny house was too small for him, as she had intimated. I thought it would be really special to live somewhere near the beloved Judge and Mayor, although I really didn't know much else about the place. I could picture myself sitting on that amazing porch hanging out with the sweet, loving Judge.

Monday night came and, about 5:00 p.m. my phone rang with a strange number from Boone, NC. I knew who it was even though that number wasn't from our town of Banner Elk. It was Brenda, the Mayor, and she said the magic words I was hoping for, "That gentleman called and said that the HOUSE WAS TOO SMALL FOR HIM!"

As I have said many times over the last few years and continue to say almost daily, **YOU CAN'T MAKE THIS STUFF UP.** But I can write it down and observe in constant amazement.

I went down the few blocks from my old apartment to view my new place, knowing for certain that it would be PERFECT. I was in a foggy, heavenly haze as I slowly, peacefully, lovingly strolled down to the Mayor's house. She showed me the incredible, historic, chapel-like, tiny A-frame house that I now live in. I loved it. I loved everything about it from the apple trees in the back to the view from the backyard of the scenic, magically, GODLY

Grandfather Mountain. The price was embarrassingly low for the market now and I can walk anywhere downtown conveniently. I am living on Main Street in my favorite town, in the kind of town I have always dreamed of living. My good fortune was, no doubt, DIVINE INTERVENTION and it was further CONFIRMATION for me that God is with us, and God is great!

As if all that wasn't gorgeously overwhelming enough, the Mayor now brought me to see the Judge, saying that he would want to "talk" to me, even though we both knew he didn't say much. The icing on the cake, as if I needed any more, was her telling my future dear friend and mentor that I was going to move in behind them. "If it's okay with you, Judge," I added.

She blew my mind with her next comment. She said, "He will sit on the porch with you when he's not working." I honestly don't recall or believe that I ever said that out loud to the Mayor, but she somehow knew that I would end up cherishing so many moments on the porch with him. God certainly knew. Going back to that time where *BE HERE NOW* pointed me to that stage of GOD, this is one of the CONFIRMATIONS that gave me the FAITH that I now hold as CERTAIN. Thank you, GOD. Thank you, UNIVERSE.

 TRY NOT TO WHINE OR COMPLAIN

I have spent the majority of my life whining and complaining about the minutiae of everyday life. This trait is a common one that many of us share. Somewhere along the line, we were taught or we picked up the notion that life is supposed to be easy, fair, or perfect. It actually can be all of those

LIVING WITH JOY, PEACE, AND HAPPINESS

things, but it won't just happen to you. It takes effort, commitment, and – most of all – an undying desire to find **HAPPINESS**. Our perspective can let it happen if we are in the right place. I have come to realize that we have far more control of our senses and our ability to stay comfortable under less than perfect conditions. We have just gotten used to complaining, whining, and aborting certain situations just because it's a little chilly or windy or maybe a little rainy. One of the ten laws of Dharma is control of one's senses. I find that we can actually handle many more of these minor discomforts if we only choose to focus on something else. Also, the words we use and our general self-talk about being tired, cold, or hot only reinforces these feelings like a self-fulfilling prophecy.

I recently arranged a last-minute kickball game in my little town for fun and to BTP (Break The Pencil). It turned out to be at about midnight on a random Sunday and the weather was certainly not ideal. It was about 50 degrees, maybe less, wet and rainy. The field was where we have the town's famed Woolly Worm Festival in October each year and I believe this kickball game happened in November. I rallied a bunch of restaurant employees from the cafe by the field, all of whom were half of my fifty years of age. They were still good to go in spite of the weather after their shift. I walked to the Pantry across the street to get some beer for the crew and myself. I waited outside in the drizzle until they closed up the restaurant. Finally, when they came out, I was so pumped for this rare special event that the wet cold atmosphere didn't bother me at all. A couple of the young girls whined about the temperature and one cried and bailed after one fall. I encouraged the others to *embrace the suck*, a military term I had recently heard and adopted. I knew that once everyone was fully engaged and in the zone, their weather-induced discomforts would fade away. I became slightly obsessed with being the last one to "eat it" in the mud as, one by one, we were all succumbing to the swampy field. We played for like two hours and it was a memorable experience that I knew I would never forget. The truth was reinforced for me that night. Perspective is hugely important in the enjoyment of life and especially in finding joy in simple experiences that can then become personally historic moments. There is a great quote by Shakespeare, "Nothing is either good or bad. Only thinking it makes it so."

I was driving in Kentucky for the first time recently and it was fairly obvious I was in a God-loving area by the amount of radio stations that were focused on religion. It was becoming increasingly evident at the time that I should study the Bible some. Most, if not all, of my accelerated spiritual growth had been from sources other than the Scriptures, including many self-help and Buddhist books and teachings. One particular southern gentleman preacher was speaking of how *Proverbs* expressed many of the same principles and sentiments that have been espoused in those very books. He chose a specific guideline that I had recently worked on, but said it beautifully as preachers often do. Don't complain, or criticize, or condemn.

DON'T COMPLAIN, DON'T CRITICIZE, DON'T CONDEMN

Mostly, I have become accustomed to omitting these behaviors from my life. What a huge difference it has made in my pure joy and happiness! I'm also pretty sure that the gravy on top or residual effect of not contributing to these common actions is that I am a much more pleasant person to be around. Isn't that a **WIN-WIN?**

LIVING WITH JOY, PEACE, AND HAPPINESS

With the long-awaited awareness of how much energy most people waste on these negative thoughts, I NOW avoid them. I don't compare the experience to some other time. I make sure to not be in that past and I **EMBRACE NOW!** The former only gives you ammunition to complain and that makes everyone miserable. The latter enhances the experience for you and everyone around you.

 TRY BEING A PEACEFUL WARRIOR

Along the same lines of the previous chapter on whining and complaining, I am training myself to use the phrase that was used throughout Dan Millman's books. I read his first two books in the *Peaceful Warrior* series back in college. I connected greatly with his concepts back then and have gone back to reread them over the years. His mysterious, motivational, and inspirational stories focus on psychology and mind training, which are areas I have continued to study deeply. The **PEACEFUL WARRIOR** represents to me the way I want to behave.

We all encounter inconveniences and frustrations in our daily lives, whether it be traffic, a moody coworker or boss, constant financial pressures, or any other challenges. I am now aware that many of us react to those difficulties by lashing out at others around us and often complete strangers. It's the old saying of

33

HINTS 4 HAPPINESS

how we "kick the cat." As an animal lover and longtime cat owner, I would never physically do such a thing, so why would I ever want to act in any way that would even appear similar? With my improved consciousness, I know that I don't. I also think the analogy is quite fair. We see people act this way almost daily in the real world. Somebody doesn't get exactly what they want, exactly in the way they want it, exactly when they demand it, and they let the person in front of them hear all about it.

Being a **PEACEFUL WARRIOR** also means not complaining about every minor inconvenience we encounter in our lives, as mentioned previously regarding our rainy kickball game. Somewhere along the line in our lives, we lose the wondrous child explorer inside us. We are taught to be afraid, and not get dirty, and so many other uptight directives that close us off to so many of life's mysteries and adventures. We cancel trips or outings because of a little iffy weather or some other slight challenge. I have begun to push myself a little more in such situations, because I now realize that beautiful experiences often emerge from these non-perfect settings.

There is also an extra amount of SATISFACTION that comes with facing these little adversities, accepting the challenge with vigor and enthusiasm, and making the MOST OF THE EXPERIENCE!!!

I had been hearing for years about a destination in Virginia called the Creeper Trail. I never knew exactly what it was, but had heard murmurs about it for a while. Finally, my good friend and *forever fiance* Amy invited me to go along with her and her sister one random Thursday afternoon. On the one-hour ride over, they described it to me as a "lazy river for bicycles," which sounded awesome to me. We were going at the peak of

LIVING WITH JOY, PEACE, AND HAPPINESS

the autumn leaf season so I knew the setting was going to be gorgeous. It was. The girls hadn't planned ahead, not expecting any trouble renting bikes midweek. It turned out that, because of Covid lockdowns throughout the country, outdoor activities like the bike trail were slammed.

Amy went to work on her cell phone trying to find us bicycles and, even more challenging, getting us a seat on a shuttle to transport us to the top of the hill. The girls were resolved to get us on bikes, so we went from store to store until we found them. We still couldn't get a shuttle ride to the top like most people do, so instead we just rode up the hill for a couple of miles. So much for the lazy river! However, it turned out perfectly. We got a little workout on the way up and the scenery was gorgeous with creeks along the way. Then, when we all decided we had pushed ourselves enough (which felt awesome in itself), we took the lovely, rewarding ride down the hill and had an awesome meal and beers at a local hangout. The day was **MAGICAL**! I enjoyed every bit of the experience. We have amazing pics marking the moment and we discuss going back often.

I was going to have fun either way. This attitude has changed my life and continues to ensure joyous adventures constantly!

HINTS 4 HAPPINESS

The **PEACEFUL WARRIOR** in me allows patience, understanding, and perspective to diffuse any situations as such that in the past would have had me behaving much like the unaware individuals I've mentioned.

Once, a student of the spiritual teacher/guru/author, Eckhart Tolle, asked him what his proudest accomplishments were. Tolle replied that it was his ability to **CONTROL HIS OWN THOUGHTS.** I fully realize how big this ability is in my own enjoyment of life. This question inspired me to answer the same question. After some pondering, I came up with this answer to my proudest accomplishment.

My proudest accomplishment is my ability to choose HAPPINESS in just about all situations, circumstances, and moments. At the very least, I know that I will be far less unhappy than most people under ANY circumstances and I will NOT lash out at others or COMPLAIN about it. I can just MAKE THE BEST OF IT, knowing that many others have dealt with FAR WORSE and, overall, I'm BEYOND BLESSED, with so much in my life at this point. As with any challenge I face, I now know, that it is just my turn to endure WHATEVER it is and I am up for the adventure and the challenge.

LIVING WITH JOY, PEACE, AND HAPPINESS

 POM (PEACE OF MIND)

Peace Of Mind is a phrase that I have heard over the years. I have started using the POM abbreviation in the last few years. It encompasses the ultimate calm and contentment that I have strived for since my youth. One morning, it became my meditation mantra. I was visiting my ailing mother in Delray Beach, Florida. She was only about 73 years old at the time, but was well along on her *oxycodone* downfall. Her apartment was not a very comfortable place to be at that time. When I would visit, I would end up on the familiar living room couch. The whole place smelled of dog urine, since her yappy little Maltese never got walked and, though there were pee pads out, she went wherever she pleased.

That one particular day, I started using **POM** as my mantra while meditating to get me into a peaceful state before I ventured out for the day. Later that afternoon, when I went to the Hard Rock Casino in Hollywood, Florida, to take my mind off things further and to feed my little gambling urge, I had several "highpiphenies" as I later coined them. I was thoroughly enjoying bonding with many people at a black jack table. Even though we were all getting our butts kicked by the dealers, I noticed luck began to turn in our direction. While I was getting paid, I happened to notice a new face standing across from us. There was a sweet-faced Asian lady dealing the cards now. I said, "I like you," since she seemed to be the first one actually paying us, for a change. I asked her name and she answered POM! This was just a few hours after I had used the acronym as my meditation word. My response was my usual one when I was shocked by another startling universal confirmation. I exclaimed "Get the f outta here!!" I then asked how it was spelled, assuming it would be some complicated Asian thing like *Phalm*, and I was even more flabbergasted when she calmly replied "P-O-M."

I go back to this meditation tool often. Once I became better and better at quieting the mind, I found many techniques to help put me in the most relaxed state to either simply give the mind a rest, fix something that is not working smoothly, or to ask the Universe for a solution. After using some methods like counting down, focusing on the letters **POM** has been very helpful in clearing away other thoughts. I also use the number 0 as a way of visualizing NOTHING. I simply picture that large 0, then even follow the shape of the ZERO as if I were drawing it or even as if I were walking or driving along the shape of this number. The same is done with the letters **POM. It gets EASIER with PRACTICE!!!**

 TRY NOT SWEATING THE SMALL STUFF

I heard this adage followed up with, "it's all small stuff" many years ago. I liked that addition to the saying but didn't truly believe it and live it till recently.

Indian Yogi Sadghuru talks about how so many of our frustrations in life are merely based on the fact that our day doesn't go exactly how we planned it. He talks about how silly it is for us to expect such when the world is constantly moving and changing. I now realize how correct he is. He also

LIVING WITH JOY, PEACE, AND HAPPINESS

mentions how boring life would be if our blueprint for the day followed that exact path at all times. There is that other saying, "We make plans and God laughs." I love that one now that I better understand the nature of our existence.

These little sidetracks seem to be some of the most BEAUTIFUL experiences ever and I now believe the key to less suffering and more joy is to embrace these moments, go with the flow, and ENJOY THE WONDER OF IT ALL!

This insight has helped me embrace any little hiccups in life from catching a red light when running late to being robbed from my safe on a recent Las Vegas trip. I was able to laugh off the latter almost immediately by understanding that it's all part of life and I now have a crazy hangover-style story to tell forever.

Like the **JOE WALSH RULE**, this adage of not "sweating the small stuff" is all about perspective. If we can just understand that these little inconveniences are beyond our control, and do actually make life more interesting, then we can choose to lessen or even eliminate the stress that we ALLOW to accompany such adventures. Then we can embrace such variations in our daily life, rather than complain about them. Treating things in this way, my friends, will add to your joy, instead of draining from it. DOES THAT MAKE SENSE?

There is also the saying, "we'll laugh about it later," and this adage is very true. We can almost always find humor in the "mini tragedies" of everyday life after time softens our anger or frustration. A wise person said, "why not laugh about it now?" Often we are so caught up in our desire for the moment, and we're accustomed to getting it in a timely manner or we throw a tantrum. Once we look back at the situation, we realize we acted stupidly, like spoiled children. If we are on the journey of personal growth, then hopefully we will improve upon our behavior the next time. If we have the perspective that so many people have REAL difficulties in life, compared with ours, we can be able to laugh about everything RIGHT NOW!!

 TRY LAUGHING OUT LOUD AND OFTEN

Now that I have found true peace in life and I feel as though I am living on purpose, smiles and laughter flow much easier on a daily basis. People often inquire what I'm laughing about or giggling over. They often assume it's something critical about them or an inside joke that they are missing. I believe that's because we learn so early in society to mock or make fun of each other. Now that I have retrained my mind to notice and observe with less judgment, these moments of laughter are just me enjoying the nature of events or actions, yet with less criticism. Usually, I am finding humor in unusual moments that just make me appreciate the weirdness of life in general and now gives me pleasure. I no longer look for reasons to criticize, but rather for ways to delight in these variations of normalcy.

There have been certain profound moments that I would consider almost paranormal. These moments are what many call *synchronicity*. On one such occasion, I was having one of those crazy, surreal nights that you cannot make up. I had ventured out looking for a dive bar in the Boca

LIVING WITH JOY, PEACE, AND HAPPINESS

Raton/Delray Beach area in Florida. I found a place called The Artful Dodger, which satisfied that desire perfectly. I met a feisty, but friendly, chick bartender that I hit it off with. Then some yuppy-like dude invited me to his car to smoke a bowl. Just when I was feeling great in my little afternoon of day drinking, escaping from the daily grind of dealing with my mom's passing, I realized that I didn't have my rental car keys. I had left them in that yuppy guy's car, apparently, and he was gone. In past times, losing my keys would have stressed me out beyond belief. This time I just asked the bartender girl to double check if she could see my keys anywhere. While the happy hour crowd started to pour in, I strolled out the door with my delightful buzz. I checked my phone, with its dying battery, to find that I was about five miles from my stepdad's apartment. Like a **PEACEFUL WARRIOR,** I headed toward my temporary home. As I was walking in the direction I hoped was the right way, my brother called to discuss Mom's funeral stuff. I quickly try to explain that my phone's about to poop out and I have about five miles to go. I know he was thoroughly confused as I hung up and I focused on the silly journey I was on. It was starting to get dark. As I was wandering through the streets of Boca, I noticed that there were no street signs. Earlier that week while I was walking through the streets near my step dad's place, I had noticed that the street names were listed on the crosswalk buttons. I looked at those metal buttons to see if I vaguely was walking in the proper direction. I could find no street names anywhere. I was lost, buzzed, slightly confused, yet thoroughly happy, joyous, and even giddy. I looked up at the skies and laughed at the uniqueness of this weird, magical moment that felt like the Universe was completely messing with me. Some people refer to this type of moment as understanding the **"COSMIC JOKE."** I was so in the moment, it was awesome. I laughed until there were joyous tears in my eyes.

HINTS 4 HAPPINESS

 TRY SPREADING ONLY JOY

Now that I have found such profound **HAPPINESS** and **JOY** in my life, although of course it is still an ever-continuing process to continue to improve, I can focus more on spreading such contentment to others. I have come to understand that not everyone is prepared to seek such happiness, so I am careful not to push my newfound methods on anyone.

I WOULD LIKE TO SHOW THE WORLD WITH MY OWN PEACEFUL, ENTHUSIASTIC WONDER THAT THIS KIND OF JOY IS, IN FACT, POSSIBLE AND CAN INDEED HAPPEN EVEN AT SUCH A MATURE AGE AS FIFTY!

Since I am very interested in letting go of the ego I have developed in life, and I'm very aware of the peace of mind that accompanies this growth, the pleasure felt from spreading joy and love to others rather than criticism has become almost euphoric. The more I have learned to control my thoughts through awareness, the happier I am each day because I can choose to think of positive things rather than the problems or concerns that are beyond my personal control.

During the Coronavirus Pandemic of 2020 there was much uncertainty and stress for the average person. In addition to the virus that has affected all humans on this Earth, there has been civil unrest throughout the United States and in some other countries because of police brutality and other racial inequality. These issues do bother me and remind me that I have been privileged to grow up in a white upper-middle-class situation, though

LIVING WITH JOY, PEACE, AND HAPPINESS

I have dealt with some prejudice as a Jewish individual. I would like nothing more than for every human of every race, creed, religion, or sexual orientation to be treated equally. I have often felt compelled to stand up for certain repressed communities and get involved in the struggle. I never got into politics in a major way because I found that was not something I wanted to pursue as a career and I had other dreams to follow. In various situations, I have stood up vigorously for people's rights in my periphery when presented with such prejudices and I am proud of those personal statements. I believe that addressing these feelings and the compassion and frustration that comes with them is necessary for certain changes to occur in society. We must individually decide which causes are most important to pursue. What creates stress, fear, and general discomfort is when people get overwhelmed by such feelings and yet don't evaluate or channel those emotions properly.

People often finish a hard day of work or, possibly worse, they start their day watching the news, which can focus mostly on the difficulties, sadness, and horrors of the world. That viewing will put people in a negative state of mind draining any joy, peace, or happiness from their consciousness. If we are going to use these feelings to create dramatic change in society, then these stirrings can be powerful and useful. In reality, very few of us are going to choose this avenue as a serious endeavor because we are busy making a living, raising a family, or with other pursuits. To watch television or Internet news or to read about such injustices while living our lives will only continue to add to the unrest and stress that we already experience in our daily activities. What does this accomplish for us? Nothing positive. In addition to our feeling angry, fearful, and sad about these issues over which we have no control or no intention of getting involved with, we then spread these frustrations to others through our negative words or interactions with strangers and our friends and family. Now we are creating an ever-expanding tidal wave of negative emotions wherever we go. This constant focus on the negative aspects of our lives creates an army of people who subscribe to a "Chicken Little" philosophy. In their world, they continuously feel like the sky is falling. Many of these unfortunates then seem to take on the responsibility of spreading their worries throughout the community. They don't even have the awareness that they are doing this. They hide behind the facade of being "a realist," when in fact it's their own fears, discontent and insecurities that fuel these concerns.

I have made the conscious decision to accomplish the exact opposite. What if everywhere I go and with everyone I come into contact with I spread peace, love, compassion and happiness like, say, Mr. Rogers did? That goal has become one of my most important missions in this life and has contributed to the profound **HAPPINESS** and joy that I now experience daily.

 CLOCK STOPPERS

My good friend Phil is a fireman from south Florida. I met him in middle school when we moved from Sarasota. Back then, he was just that Mordente kid from PE class, but moving thirty years forward, he has become one of my most important friends. Phil and his lovely wife Colette started this little trip to the Keys back in the late nineties. I was fortunate enough to be invited on one of these early road trips and I have no doubt that it changed the trajectory of my life. No matter what struggle or challenge that was

LIVING WITH JOY, PEACE, AND HAPPINESS

happening in my life, the Keys trip gave me a yearly escape from all of those worries. Phil guided me on these Keys trips. He showed many of us how to slow down, relax, and smell the **ROSES OF LIFE**. I can picture him sniffing life with his arms wide open and breathing deeply. A couple of years, ago we came up with *clock stopper* as a way to describe that feeling when we appreciate the moment and mark how wonderful and short life is.

In my little town, we have a clock tower at the stoplight downtown. It was erected a few years ago on the corner lot where a legendary bar and restaurant used to be. There is a pretty little sitting area with benches and a row of hedges. I love this quaint spot and I often stop by there on my two-block walk home from the village. What I also thoroughly enjoy are the chimes that emanate from the clock each half hour and especially on the hour when you are reminded what time it is by the number of tones that ring out and can be heard from my tiny house. I use these sounds as a reminder to appreciate and be grateful for another hour of life.

It has been said that about a quarter million people die in the world each day. When we put that in perspective along with the understanding of how fast life seems to pass, especially as we grow older, then it now seems obvious to me that I should feel blessed for each and every hour that goes by.

Acknowledging this good fortune not only acts as a way of slowing down the quickly-turning pages of life's book, but also it reminds us to not waste time with worry, whining, or "woe is me."

You don't need the clock or its bells to "slow down time." Of course, we can't technically slow down time as far as we can prove yet, but I have been able to stop myself from getting caught up in compulsivity by reminding myself to be in the moment. I might be rushing home from work, (walking usually) for no real reason, other than the active energy still flowing from the job.

I'll just STOP, look up at the sky, notice all my surroundings that I had been ignoring in my "sleep walking" rush home. And then I'M BACK IN THE MOMENT, SLOWLY ENJOYING THE SHORT WALK HOME. Yes, it CAN BE DONE, DAILY…AND THROUGHOUT EACH DAY AND LIFE THIS WAY…Is GLORIOUS, I must say. (Sorry, I do like to rhyme and write songs on the side.)

 ## TRY TO BE LIKE MATHIEU

Mentors in life are extremely important. When we are young, mentoring starts with our parents, siblings, neighbors, teachers, friends, and coaches. Then it morphs into other people we come across in life through our jobs and other interactions in public. If we are fortunate, we are led to great mentors who set us on a proper path. They encourage and comfort us in challenging times. Hopefully, someone sees the potential in us and has the caring and patience to guide us, even though we may be difficult in uncertain times of growth. Sometimes we choose the wrong people to follow, which can retard our advancement or even plunge us into trouble or darkness. Mostly, I have been blessed in this case, for generally I have found wonderful role models from whom to learn such as authors and motivators like **Anthony Robbins, Dr. Wayne Dyer,** and **Zig Ziglar**. I also read **Dale Carnegie** and eventually was given a book by the incredible **Ram Dass**, *BE HERE NOW*. Recently, I discovered a Buddhist monk named **MATHIEU RICARD**. The peaceful, joyous Mathieu is noted to be the happiest man in the world. He downplays this finding as all great spiritual guides would, but to watch him speak removes any doubt of his equanimity and joy. Much like with the much-revered **Dalai Lama,** another guide and mentor to me, one can feel the profound level of peace. Mr. Ricard's brain shows signs of pure happiness at a higher level than any other brain studied. I knew upon hearing this determination that he would be one to emulate. Again, going back to something that Mr. Robbins taught in his book *Unlimited Power*, we don't have to solve the mysteries on our own. My number one mission or goal in life became finding **HAPPINESS**, so who else should I follow other than the happiest man in the world? I initially figured I would try to be happier than him, but then I realized that just to be in his "neighborhood" would be WONDERFUL. I'm now fairly confident that that's exactly where I reside.

IT'S <u>ALWAYS</u> A BEAUTIFUL DAY IN THIS NEIGHBORHOOD
Now that I have thoroughly studied people like Mr. RICARD and many other people, up close and far away, and learned the many tools and techniques that lead to **HAPPINESS**, I am prepared to show these methods and their possibilities to the world. Hopefully, by doing so I can actually help make the world a HAPPIER PLACE! To quote one of my favorite and happiest

bands, The Beach Boys, "WOULDN'T IT **BE NICE?**"

 A FEW OF MY FAVORITE COMPLIMENTS

It's amazing how life can change once your perspective improves dramatically. Instead of little altercations with strangers or even friends, they say nice things about you, right to you! It's wonderful. At first, it's almost off-putting or uncomfortable because it doesn't feel normal. But now, it's incredible how special and cherished these little comments can be. I don't need them or expect them, which makes them that much more heart-warming when they come at you.

Someone I work with said, "You are the cheeriest person I've ever met." Another one said, "You're always in a great mood. I don't get it." My stepfather said, "You're the least judgmental person I've ever met." These compliments or observations from those around me hint that, though there's certainly plenty of room for more improvement, I seem to be on the right path. Another comment that I enjoyed was from a coworker who said, "Craig treats everyone the same." Another cohort gave me what I call the best compliment with the worse grammar. He called me the "unfakest" person he knows!

In this world I have witnessed people who kiss up to the owners and bosses or anyone who can help their career or offer some other reward for such behavior and then berate or talk down to those whom they feel are their inferiors. I am proud to be known for respecting everyone equally. Probably the greatest compliment I have ever gotten came from a young girl with whom I work after I caught a moth inside to free it outside. She said, **"You are too good for this world."** It would be tough to beat that one, and coming from that extremely kind, sweet, young girl, it meant so much.

ENJOY THE DAY

Looking back, it seems I have had many battles within myself: money versus poor; type A, all business versus fun; strong and asshole-ish versus sensitive, compassionate, and kind.

After so many years of balancing both, I finally realized that my true inner self wants to be all the positives. I am more comfortable, at peace and happier in the latter. Money doesn't matter. Maybe I went so hard on the negatives that I got it out in the middle thirty-five years or so. Along with the complaining, entitlement and general negativity, I finally annoyed myself into changing. It is a choice everyone ultimately can make, once we realize we can **control our own thoughts** and we work at it enough to do it consistently, daily, even momentarily.

This next statement is going to be nearly impossible for most people to believe or comprehend, but those who know me personally would absolutely back me up. **I don't have bad days anymore**.

A few years back, I started keeping track on my wall calendar of my good and bad days. I came up with a little system with different color markers where I would put a symbol of some kind on each day that represented what kind of day it had been. For instance, an exceptionally happy day would get a smiley face. An unhappy or especially frustrating day would get a frown. Also, I would evaluate my own behavior almost like giving myself a report card. If I acted badly, which usually involved losing my temper and saying something mean to someone, I would give that day a red X. I came up with an explanation for each symbol so I could properly evaluate myself as well as explain my methods to others. The definition of a good day that received a smiley face was that I thought and spoke positively for more than fifty percent of that day. The frown represented a negative attitude for more than fifty percent of that day. Before I started monitoring these things, I think I was probably positive about fifty to seventy-five percent of the time, but the intensity of my negativity caused a huge amount of discomfort and anger. Documenting such specific criteria about each day gave me great insight and allowed me to stand back, evaluate, and then make the necessary changes.

SADGHURU talks about how important it is to keep track of your personal growth. He notes how diligent most of us are when accounting for money and business, yet negligent in documenting these spiritual advancements or digressions. I now can see a direct correlation between my journaling these behaviors and the improvements that followed in my growth and my overall joy of life. I started to make goals about how few bad days were possible and how many happy, joyous, and extraordinary days were reasonable. Initially, less than five bad days a month seemed unreachable. Then my behavior towards others and even life in general improved to gain on my goals. Then I hoped for only one or two tough days a month, so that I could minimize them to under 24 per year. That seemed like a pretty happy universe considering I used to have at least a couple of negative days in each week. Now that so few things upset me or take me away from happiness, even days with funerals or unexpected tragedy can be, weirdly, pretty magical days. It's the perspective that has changed. If I live on purpose, with altruism, peace, and love in my heart and stay congruent with my actions, then those challenges that occur in life that are beyond our control can be handled with equanimity.

 DEALING WITH PHYSICAL PAIN AND DISCOMFORT

This topic came to mind recently because of some weird physical maladies that have come my way. I won't bore you or belabor over medical stuff that those people my age seem to revel in, but let's just say I've spent some time in bed of late. Just after talking about how I don't have bad days, I feel compelled to explain how the physical aspect can be challenging at times.

The Buddhist attitude towards most physical pain and discomfort is that it's just a body. Many believe we can "separate" the mind, body, and soul enough to be able to minimize, if not eliminate, most pains by doing so. I do believe this feat is likely possible in most cases, although I think it takes much practice and possibly expertise in meditation and other healing techniques. I have not achieved that level of practice yet, but I have continued to work on it throughout any physical challenges I have faced. I have definitely found some level of comfort with some meditations during these times. I also am working on other distraction methods to lessen the mind's focus on the pain when it is prevalent. It's like when I tease the many complainers I encounter who must loudly speak of any level of discomfort they encounter. They will whine that it's cold, it's hot, I'm tired, I'm bored, or my _____ hurts.

HINTS 4 HAPPINESS

I usually remind the person whining, "You know what's not gonna make you less cold/ hot/ tired? That you're talking about it and focusing on it!"

At an Anthony Robbins seminar back in 1990-something, I was fortunate enough to get a one-on-one experience with the physical and psychological giant. He stands about 6'7", yet his presence makes him seem even larger. I speak and write of his definition of charisma, which I love.

Charisma is when others feel good about themselves and you.

Tony Robbins embodies this trait. On stage or screen, he's large. Up close and personal, he's monumental. When he asked for a volunteer for a particular exercise out of a crowd of 3,500 people, my two buddies yelled my name. Tony heard them and said, "This guy's got a fan club," so he chose me to come up on stage with him. This section of the amazing, life-changing, fire-walking, *Awaken the Giant Within Seminar*, in Orlando, was on being able to affect your pain or discomfort positively with your mind. He was showing us how. His method, with me on stage in a chair, was gently to talk me into a state where I felt pain or pleasure and then show how we can change those by coaching our mind through it. Basically, the walking of the fire, etc., was all about using **mind over matter,** although I remember he didn't like that phrase. Sorry, Tony.

So, when he helped me get back into the state of mind and pain I was in when I blew out my knee in college, he used a sort of psychotherapy method. First, he talked me into experiencing a romantic situation. I deeply imagined everything I felt with all senses during that ecstasy moment. When he got me to feel like I was back in it at a scale of one hundred percent after a joke about not going too far, he had me describe specifically where I felt soooo good. I had a big, happy, smile. Then, after that, he had me relive the time that I tore three ligaments in my knee. I knew my pain was showing on my face and body language for the seminar audience. Then he coached me on changing the pain, heat, heaviness, and pressure on my knee to a light, cool, pleasant sensation in that area. He then guided me to change my focus from the knee to my romantic areas and reminded me of the pleasure I felt back in that ecstasy moment. He was showing us we could control our focus to ease the pain. It absolutely worked on stage. The experience was MAGICAL.

WHATEVER YOU FOCUS YOUR MIND ON EXPANDS

So, let's go back to the concept of having no bad days. Some of these recent days I've dealt with some pretty heavy physical discomfort to where I actually stayed home on a day off rather than going exploring or creating some MAGICAL new experience. Would these days get a 10 or 10-plus on the SCALE OF HAPPINESS? Maybe not. But I do believe that my conscious work on not letting some physical pain or limitation ruin a day off has been accomplished by an overall positive perspective. Rather than adding to any physical annoyance by dwelling in self-pity or frustration, I just think of it as my time to rest for whatever reason, and how I can make the best of this downtime. Also, there is my friend Sensei Bob's mantra, "What can I learn from this?" Often, I think of how this experience I'm going through might benefit someone else later in life, as I know I will be able to impart what I am learning from it. All of these ideas upon which I choose to focus help keep my SCALE OF HAPPINESS number at a solid 8 or higher, even in the face of multiple forms of physical discomfort. When the physical pain or discomfort subsides, as I hope it will for people always, it is so EASY to be back up to a 10 or 10-plus, since you just got past some of those annoying conveniences. GRATEFULNESS then can and should be ABUNDANT!

 ## CREATING THE PERFECT DAY

Going with the flow of life can be challenging, especially when we have been told throughout our lives not to be lazy. What you were told probably depends greatly on your upbringing or other surroundings. The more we get in touch with our inner selves and become in touch with the Universe, the more instinctively we are led to know what is needed or right for each day. Sometimes, the perfect day is hanging around the house and being lazy. In this case, we might have to deal with inner voices nagging at us to get up and "Do something" or maybe a spouse complaining. Then we might go through a process of defending ourselves as to why we deserve a quiet, inactive day at home. At this point, I remind myself not to attach to that inner critical voice and instead listen to my wiser self who knows that it's perfectly okay to chill at home for the day. On other days, the sense

LIVING WITH JOY, PEACE, AND HAPPINESS

of adventure is on fire and I can't wait to roam around and see what is in store for the morning, afternoon, or evening. Being aware of that flow, and then following its course, becomes second nature and wonderful.

Just the other day I chose to embrace the wonder of the day and followed that mantra for the afternoon. I also have thought of it as creating a painting for the day. There is no right or wrong answer for the outcome. Just enjoy the mystery of it. Balance is the key here. As much as I have an awareness that our physical body is just a vehicle for our journey, much like a rental car, it is important to be in tune with our body and give it rest when needed.

Consciousness also gives us a sense of when to sit out or take some quiet time to balance the adventures that add to our life experience. The term FOMO, which stands for "fear of missing out," can be a real thing for many people. I used to suffer from this fear and be guided by this when choosing my free time activities. Now that I have a great time in any situation, I am easily led by my spiritual intuition and I'm comfortable with each and every outcome.

Once I realized how important personal connection is, I have a new understanding of how amazing some "small" moments can be. Now that I also feel this connection with the Universe, I can FEEL the importance of many of these quieter experiences. Sometimes it's just having a moment with someone outside of your normal acquaintance with them, like the first time you have a drink with a coworker away from the job. It can even be a funeral, like I've discussed, where you just know that this is where you're supposed to be. Often, this feeling is because you know your support is required there or maybe just out of respect to the departed one, you **NEED**

to be there.

Then, there are moments when your sense of community and the ones who I call "chosen family" are with you. You may be in a setting that is incredibly peaceful and homey, or even in an **intense** moment in life. Yet, whatever the situation, you feel you **belong** there. These are the moments when I refer to the beautiful song, ***"Right here, right now, there isn't any other place, I'd rather be!"***

 ## WAKING UP SPIRITUALLY

Many gurus and authors have tried to assist their followers and readers through the awakening process. It is certainly a humble hope for this book as well. I have looked back over my own transformation, which seems to have occurred over the past few years. Many different events happened that led to my current awareness, which caused significant changes in my personality and focus. It was like a series of events that were brought to my attention and culminated in a realization that something major had occurred. This Realization Day was in July, 2019. As mentioned previously, while reading *BE HERE NOW*, I began to receive clarity from a chain of events that would change my perspective and open my eyes to a belief in God.

One of my first recollections of experiences, which led me to believe that something bigger and magical was happening in life, was a mystical white crow that lived in Banner Elk. I had heard of the mysterious, rare bird about a year before I had the privilege of viewing her. Several people had spoken

LIVING WITH JOY, PEACE, AND HAPPINESS

of the existence of this amazingly rare white crow. After hearing about her for a while, it became my mission to locate her. The chef, family member and owner of the Italian restaurant where I worked told me that the bird hung out at the end of her road almost every morning. Since this location was only about a half mile from my apartment and right on the way to our convenient Dollar General, I was hot on the trail to see her. I was diligent in my search for about a month until it finally happened.

It was a lovely St. Patrick's Day, on a Tuesday I think, which at that time was my day off. I had loosely planned a day of barhopping through town. My aforementioned ex-military friend, Jay, came to meet me at the Barra, the sports bar connected to that Italian restaurant. I was the bartender Wednesday through Sunday. We started our Irish celebration there and

HINTS 4 HAPPINESS

then walked about a quarter of a mile to the local brewery, which happened to be right in the center of the four-block area that the crow was known to frequent. We were enjoying some local beers inside when one of us mentioned the magical bird.

Jay and I were about to move to the next destination and we exited the building. My other good buddy and neighbor, whom I refer to as YUKON CORNELIUS because of his resemblance to the cartoon character from the *Rudolph Christmas Special*, said he had just seen the rare crow! I was already amazed by the fact that we had just spoken of her inside and not within Yukon's hearing.

Then, as if on cue, Jay exclaimed, "There it is! I just saw it!"

He pointed to her, and there she was! We all remember our first sighting. It's impossible to properly describe the feeling that accompanied this moment. It's like the childlike moment when you first saw_____. You can fill in the blank with any of your firsts growing up or beyond. This sighting might not seem all that miraculous to you, but then, of course, after seeing the beautiful Ivery, as we named her, I wanted more. I wanted pictures and then video of the super rare phenomenon. Pictures I got okay, although she was elusive at first. Then one day, I found her in one of her favorite spots on this lawn where she often hung out. I was in my car when I spotted her, so I nervously grabbed my phone and took a video as I watched her and her posse of black crows frolicking in front of my car.

I was so excited to get the video and I rushed into work to show my fellow Ivery fans what I had gotten. When I got to the restaurant to show the chef Nicole my video just about ten minutes after my encounter, the video was blacked out! You could hear the Crows cawing, but the footage was so dark that you couldn't make anything out. It just didn't make sense. I felt the magical crow was "playing" with me as was the Universe and maybe God, too.

I still have this stunning video. Later, I did get some actual video of the gorgeous creature. My friends and I had many other sightings of her that always warmed our hearts. We all knew that we were on borrowed time with her. I also felt how special it was that she could go anywhere in the world and had chosen our amazing little town for about fifteen years. When I noticed she wasn't around anymore, about a year ago, I had the most vivid and beautiful dream where she actually flew onto my shoulder in front of much of the town. I believe she was saying goodbye to me. Six months after her disappearance, I ran into a local guy who had just spotted her that day. I rushed to find Nicole, who was a crucial member of our unofficial White Crow Committee. Of course, Nic was right there in plain sight outside when I looked for her. I told her the news. I told her this Randy guy had just seen her flying away from town. She opened her mouth wide and proclaimed that she had just dreamed of Ivery the **night before**!

Everyone, of course, needs to interpret these events for himself, but I just don't believe this and other phenomena like it are COINCIDENCES. Someone said, "Coincidences are God's way of staying anonymous." I like that.

TRY RECONNECTING WITH YOUR INNER CHILD

I had an old picture from my childhood when I was about four. I was wearing this light blue jumpsuit thing with white leather shoes. It was quite a look my mother had me sporting. I clearly remember the story that accompanied this picture. Mom told of how we were headed to the city (NYC) for dinner or something. The neighbor kids were enjoying their little wading pool. I supposedly wanted to swim rather than go to the city. Although Mom told me no, emphatically, she apparently turned her head long enough for me to override her decision and I ended up in the pool in my silly new outfit, shoes and all. I had heard the story for years and, of course, snickered about my rebelliousness. Now that picture and tale have taken on new meaning. After maybe growing up too fast in some ways and becoming so rigid and uptight for so many years, I know I have reconnected with that spontaneous, fun, unwavering inner child that was so evident in that four-year-old me. I welcome that childish soul in me who now exhibits himself daily through singing, smiling, exploring, wondering, wandering, watching, and even dancing.

I HONESTLY BELIEVE THAT MY SOUL IS MORE CONNECTED WITH MY FOUR- OR FIVE-YEAR-OLD SELF THAN WITH ANY OTHER AGE. IMAGINE WHAT IT WOULD FEEL LIKE TO LIVE WITH THE PURE JOY OF A FOUR-YEAR-OLD!

The beauty of reconnecting with my inner child is that memories seem to have come back to me. When I was in summer camp as a kid, I could be moody and maybe a little spoiled. I thoroughly disliked certain activities and I'm sure I whined about them plenty. What I do remember loving at camp, much like recess in school were the times when we had a choice of several different activities. Maybe it was just the feeling of having some kind of control in a life full of school and things I had to do. The choice list back in the day might have looked something like the following: canoe rides, arts & crafts, nature walk, swimming, and capture the flag. I would almost always choose CAPTURE THE FLAG!

Now, on my days off from work, I make a similar list that might look like this: feed the ducks and lunch at the Café, hike up on the Blue Ridge Parkway and then have a couple of beers at the Pedalin' Pig, go to the Boone library and walk around King Street, find a new waterfall, feed Blacky the white horse, and go by THE STATION in Tennessee.

It's fun to have all these choices and then look for some sign to guide me. Then, no matter what choice I make, I go for it with GUSTO and I ALWAYS enjoy the EXPERIENCE.

 TRY LIVING LIKE YOU'RE DYING

I have to give a shoutout to country singer Tim McGraw who helped make this phrase more famous. There is profound beauty to this philosophy, so I try to remind myself to enjoy life this much. It is absolutely possible not to take our time on Earth for granted, but it's not necessarily easy. Sadghuru addressed this topic in one of his mini lectures that touched me well. He talked of how we should thoroughly understand how mortal we are. He said if we remember daily that our time is short and therefore priceless, and that we are all dying from the moment we are born, then we can live fully and appreciate more moments. We can then be inspired to embrace life enthusiastically, voraciously, gratefully, and joyously. Also, this leads us back to that great Beatles' tune that echoes the motto I have adopted, *"**LIFE IS VERY SHORT, THERE IS NO TIME FOR FUSSING AND FIGHTING, MY FRIEND!**"*

Many people need to have a near death experience or go through some other traumatic experience to appreciate how fragile life can be. For me, it was a combination of several factors, including losing my father when he was a relatively young 58 years old. Then, losing my financial nest egg, my mother, and several very close friends guided me to appreciate life more and be grateful for each day. When a decision comes up about whether to partake in some adventure that might be a strain financially or otherwise, I will usually embrace the word **YES!** I don't think we were put here to stay on the sideline. ***Put me in coach, I'm ready to play TODAY!***

Again, like **Breaking The Pencil** and living fully in the movie *Yes Man*, living **like you are dying** teaches us to experience our time on earth fully, enthusiastically, adventurously, and being all in on **enjoying life every day.**

 TRY SINGING OUT LOUD

On my job as bartender, I have worked tremendously on having fun and staying upbeat throughout my shift, in spite of many stressors that come along each day. These challenges can range from a difficult boss to lazy coworkers and, of course. rude, entitled and obtuse customers who often chide us like we're naughty step-children. I recently have found that singing aloud to music allows me to be in the moment, enjoy my time and express peace and happiness throughout the day. I also have determined that it is nearly impossible to hold on to a negative thought or criticism while belting out a happy favorite song. We also know that certain endorphins are released within us to improve our mood even further. The only downside to this method is that my voice needs a lot of improvement, so I hope not to offend my customers or coworkers with my lack of tonality. My sincere hope is that my singing will get better, while in the meantime, I think and hope that people will appreciate the enthusiasm and joy that I am constantly expressing with my bad singing! I want this joy and free expression to be contagious and inspire others to feel similarly. I recently heard someone ask, "Do you sing to get to the end of the song?" A great question, which might

remind us to enjoy life and not take ourselves or anything else so seriously and again to **BE IN THE MOMENT, HERE AND NOW!**

Now when I am working behind the bar, I constantly am singing out loud. I get all kinds of reactions from customers. The upbeat people seem to thoroughly enjoy it, sometimes joining in with me or commenting on my spirit. The negative folks or *buzz kill* people make disparaging comments about my voice. It has become so easy to see and feel those who embrace life versus those who muddle through it reluctantly and bitterly. I like to say that some people live in Misery Land, while we optimists prefer Disneyland or, like me, choose the **MAGIC KINGDOM!**

LIVING WITH JOY, PEACE, AND HAPPINESS

TRY TO NOT WORRY WHAT OTHERS THINK

LET ME REPEAT THIS. **Try hard – because it is hard – but keep trying not to worry about what others think!**

Often, people say they don't care what other people think. Not to do so is nearly impossible. Those of us who are part of any kind of community are bound to have a desire or even a need to be liked, respected, appreciated, or at least not hated. In my younger, more insecure, less aware days, this desire caused me plenty of worry and stress. There is, of course, still a hope that I am thought of fondly by my friends, neighbors, workmates and community acquaintances. Now that I have found comfort and more ease with my true nature and I am confident that my intentions are pure and for the greater good, I am far less concerned with what people think. I very much want to be known for strong character traits, including kindness, honesty, compassion, loyalty, and fairness.

One of my favorite compliments to receive is, "You're a good guy." It is extremely important for me to be just that. I want people to know I care and I truly want what's best for everyone. Now that I know that my behavior is congruent with these beliefs, it is less important what others think, especially when the source is considered. Some people reflect their unhappiness on those who are acting righteously. My awareness of such transference prevents me from accepting their misguided projections. Living as free, introspective, and joyous as I do can invite certain headshaking, judgment, or confusion. I don't expect or require others to comprehend my actions, so I have heard descriptions of myself as eccentric, childish, out there, or goofy. I thoroughly embrace and, per Garfield the cat, "resemble" those remarks. I have even told my brother and a couple of my closest confidants that my future behaviors may seem ridiculous or irrational. I asked them just to examine whether my actions are ultimately altruistic or benevolent. If not, then they can judge me, approach me, or even try to stop me. But if my intentions are for the greater good, then they need to sit back, watch, shake their heads or *whateva*! Meanwhile, enjoy THE SHOW!

Around the time of my last birthday, there were two interesting situations that arose regarding my newer, freer way of life. This one afternoon, I was hanging out on the porch with the Judge. As usual, I had some music playing for us, and I was happily in the mood to sing along. The Judge often would smile and even giggle while watching me be free and joyous, along with the music. This particular day, it began raining, which did the opposite of dampening my enthusiasm and spirit. The song "Shout," by Tears for Fears, played on my phone next. It was one of my "let loose and scream" anthems from high school. I could no longer contain my joy, I instinctively ran off the porch and onto the grass lawn in front. I danced and sang in the rain, certainly nowhere as good as, but lovingly reminiscent of Gene Kelley in *Dancing in the Rain.*

After the Judge and I enjoyed that MOMENT, I went back to my little house and was just chilling in my underwear when the police came to my door. It was the campus policemen from Lees-McRae College, the little college across the street from the Judge and the Mayor's compound. I threw on some clothes and greeted the officers. They said that the students at the college student center across the way had seen some guy running in between the houses or something. They asked if I had seen him.

LIVING WITH JOY, PEACE, AND HAPPINESS

I said, "I am that guy!" I told them how I was singing and dancing for the Judge. I assured them I was fully clothed and asked if doing so was against the law or something.

They were nothing but friendly, if a little perplexed. They just said that the kids were concerned.

So, I said, "Please just let them know that I live with a level of joy that is fairly uncommon, but not to worry and thank them."

Not only do I not have hard feelings about this incident, but I'm rather proud that my joy is SO elevated that it CONCERNS people. However, a part of me feels bad for those who can't even comprehend this kind of free, peaceful comfort, and contentment. I was like them, too, and now it is part of my purpose to help others find this joy if they are open to receiving it.

In a span of just a few days, there was another incident of less happy people pointing out my SILLINESS. I had full ownership of my vehicle for the first time ever. It was nothing special and kind of boring actually, my 2010 white Ford Escape with over 100,000 miles on it. With my newfound extra-free spirit soaring, this SUV, which has been very reliable and awesome in snow, just was not fun looking enough – so I painted it myself! God bless Bob Ross, and my great friend and amazingly talented Bolivian artist, David Banegas, who inspired me with his painting, spirit, and dear friendship. **The JOY OF PAINTING took me over!**

Little by little, I painted each panel of my car. Because I consider myself a **born-again hippy,** I made each panel a different color. Around town, it is

HINTS 4 HAPPINESS

obviously quite noticed. My friends all tell me they smile when they see it. I'm pretty HAPPY with that. It has been called several fun names, which I love, from "Herbie, the Love Bug" to the "clown car," to the "Rubik's Cube." The last one I heard was from a lady who said her granddaughter called it the "rainbow car." Awwwwww, that kind of melts my heart!

A few days after the police incident at my home, some people at work mentioned that a picture of my **hippy car** was on Facebook. I had dropped off Facebook many years ago for multiple reasons, not the least of which was the criticism and hatred that gets posted daily. I'm now often the last one to get the judgmental social media gossip, which ultimately leads to me being HAPPIER than the average bear! (Like Yogi, who's "smarter" than the average bear!) The Facebook post was by a good friend who, let's say, is still struggling with her own peace of mind. Her comment with the picture was, "Has anybody checked on Craig?" Then one of my best friends and fellow Buddha philosopher followed up with, "Maybe a wellness check is needed." These posts made me smile. To quote yet another song, "*IT LOOKS LIKE I'M INTO SOMETHING RIGHT!*"

I discovered over the last few years that the people who are the least

LIVING WITH JOY, PEACE, AND HAPPINESS

HAPPY, caused by a lower level of consciousness, are most annoyed by those of us who have discovered our inner joy. So, in this case and those similar, people who do not appreciate and comprehend my contentment actually act as a **universal confirmation** that I am **exactly where I need to be on this journey!**

 TRY TO MINIMIZE OR EVEN ELIMINATE WORRYING

What good does it do? ABSOLUTELY NOTHING, to quote the song. I read more than once that **97 percent** of what we worry about does not come to fruition, at least not in the catastrophic way we usually envision when we're caught up in stress and fear. Things do happen in life that are not in perfect accordance with our plans or desires, but that is inevitable. The real key is how we react to those imperfections.

BEING HAPPY DOESN'T MEAN EVERYTHING'S PERFECT.
IT MEANS YOU'VE DECIDED TO LOOK PAST
THE IMPERFECTIONS.

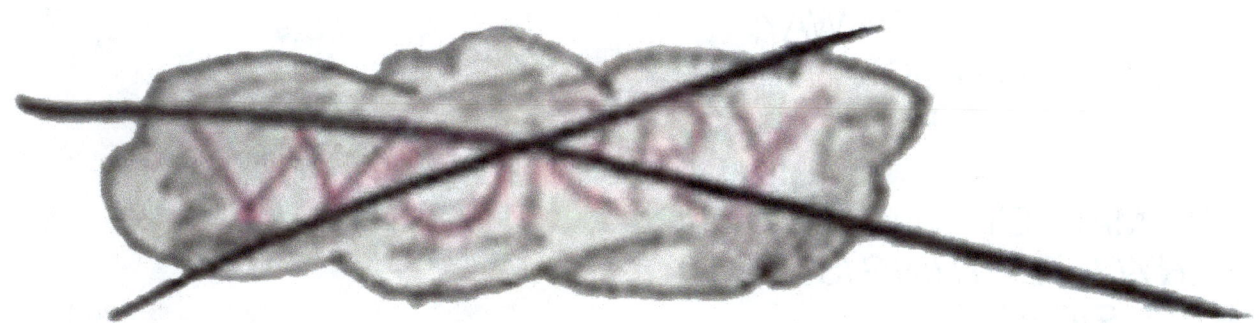

HINTS 4 HAPPINESS

As Sadghuru reminds us, life would be totally boring and monotonous if everything went exactly as planned. Aren't some of our greatest memories, adventures, and stories enhanced by weird or unexpected happenings that caused some havoc, but ultimately led to incredible outcomes and experiences? We have been gifted with this wondrous, amazing, creative imagination, which has allowed us as human beings to invent, engineer, manufacture, and create so many things to make life easier, yet we end up using this imagination against ourselves in thinking of the worst possible things that can happen to us and often we dwell in these fears. We have to relearn and teach ourselves that such obsessive worrying only keeps us from being IN THE MOMENT, and prevents us from enjoying our quiet time or other activities.

The Dalai Lama says that If there is something you can do about an issue, then don't worry. You will fix it. If there is nothing you can do about the problem, then WHY WORRY?

SO, EITHER WAY, WORRYING ABOUT IT IS POINTLESS!

BOB MARLEY was so right. *EVERY LITTLE THING IS GONNA BE ALL RIGHT!!!*

LIVING WITH JOY, PEACE, AND HAPPINESS

 ## TRY WATCHING AND LISTENING TO HAPPY THINGS

Look for things that make you feel **GOOD** and not things that anger and frustrate you. We have all met people who seem to look for reasons to be miserable. I once dated a girl who did so and she also had family members who lived this way. The ex-girlfriend probably would be considered bipolar, although one diagnosis from a therapist was *borderline personality disorder*. Whatever the label given, the fact was she had some very high and exuberant moments, which were delightful to be around, yet they were often followed or preceded by intensely dramatic episodes that caused her and those around her severe dismay. For me, the boyfriend, it became like a roller coaster ride. I could often see or feel the downturn coming, but like an oncoming freight train, I could not stop it as hard as I tried.

I used to describe those people as ones who liked or needed drama in their lives. Now I believe that they were, and some still are, just ill-equipped to properly handle or control their negative emotions. I certainly have had those issues at times as well, although maybe less often and less intense as those examples.

My introspection and studies have shown me that, with awareness, these moments can be controlled much better and even prevented altogether. What we focus on is a huge factor in overcoming these episodes and this often starts with the things we watch or listen to on a daily basis. If we focus on depressing news about the world or listen to music that puts us in a sour or sad mood, we are far more likely to be pulled into negativity than

HINTS 4 HAPPINESS

if we choose inspiring or beautiful stories to soothe our souls. Having this knowledge has allowed me to prepare myself daily by feeding my mind with nourishing stimuli rather than negative noise that may cause worry or unrest before I even encounter another person. This choice puts me in a much better place to spread positivity and kindness throughout the day.

I consciously choose more uplifting shows to watch instead of dramas on television. I guess many people like to view other people going through difficulties and tragedies to feel better about their own lives. People often ask me if I'm watching whatever drama is the most popular at the time. I usually respond with something like, "There is enough drama in the real world."

I prefer to watch lighter fare or shows with animals or documentaries that stimulate my mind as opposed to intense murder mysteries that can't help but make one feel suspicious of other humans. For a while, I got very involved in the extremely well done, entertaining HBO show *Ray Donovan*. Yes, the writing is excellent, the acting is superb, and the plot lines are intense. At the end of that hour, I found myself emotionally exhausted. Sometimes, we might feel like that's just what we need, but most times I'd rather watch the *Andy Griffith Show,* or other oldies like *Three's Company*. I know this sounds Pollyanna-like, but I do think choosing more positive programming can affect our overall psyche and even our level of happiness.

Why do people say not to watch horror shows before bed? It is because what we focus on expands in our mind. So, if you start your brain spinning on *Law And Order* or *CSI* and other shows about MURDER, where do you think your mind will go when you lie down to dream? I fully believe that part

LIVING WITH JOY, PEACE, AND HAPPINESS

of my staying in my "HAPPY PLACE" (to quote Tinkerbell from *Peter Pan)* is what I feed my mind to watch, listen to, or focus on throughout the day.

 ## ANYTHING EXCEPT POLITICS OR RELIGION

Now that I have made the conscious and continuous decision to allow my optimistic self to shine brightly, it has become very easy to recognize those people who choose the complete opposite approach. Very often these people fall back on politics as their main source of conversation. I constantly try to dodge these discussions and to avoid these people whenever possible. Politics seems to be the outlet for those who are unhappy in their lives for one reason or another. It's as if they are looking for an argument to let out the stress. They seem to hope some stranger will disagree with them or, if they find common politics with someone, then they want to bash the other side together. Either way, the conversation is negative, hateful, and divisive. Sometimes, rather than avoid these types completely like I used to, I will try to guide them gently off the argumentative political view and show that we can have common ground about much more positive topics. Some of my favorites that allow more connectedness with others are movies, music, and adventures in travel. Also, just trading stories can be what bonds us to others. Whether it's a positive experience for others depends on your openness to **LISTENING** and whether your conversation makes them feel better or worse about things after you leave them. My conscious goal is to have them feel **WAY better.**

HINTS 4 HAPPINESS

 TRY HANGING OUT WITH THE HAPPY

A huge part of keeping your surroundings upbeat and positive is choosing carefully the people with whom you spend time. I have finally learned that I can put up with, or get along with, just about everybody at work or in other certain social situations. This ability can definitely be difficult with those who have completely different values and thoughts but, as we learn to judge less, hopefully we are more accepting and, therefore, more patient and compassionate with such people. Living in a small community has taught me that we don't have to be "besties" with everyone, but there is no reason to have enemies or make others with whom you don't see eye to eye feel bad or less important because of those differences. We can all coexist peacefully if we all improve a little in this area. I am proud to note that I have nobody alive whom I would consider an adversary or enemy. That being said, there are some people who focus on negativity and live under a dark cloud consistently. I often try to encourage those types softly and compassionately. After a few attempts at doing so, when I realize they are just too comfortable in their misery to change, I stay polite but I keep my distance from them.

There is one guy in our town who completely fits this profile of the "sad sack" or Charlie Brown-type character. For people like this, it becomes the defining trait of their personality or persona. The amazing thing is that they don't completely understand how this trait affects how they are perceived by their neighbors. They subconsciously know this but they can't face it enough to make the necessary changes. I too, was that person before it

LIVING WITH JOY, PEACE, AND HAPPINESS

was brought to my attention enough times to make me **NEED** to change. For this one guy in town, I often tried to encourage him while he constantly spoke of his woes. After several times of this same scenario, I avoided sitting right next to him. One day he was extra bummed and he commented on my Florida Gator floppy hat. He was a Georgia Bulldog guy. Next thing I knew, he was wearing that old hat, which had great sentimental value to me since I had bought it outside the Swamp, the Florida Gators' football stadium at my *alma mater*. I used that moment to show him I trusted and respected him. I told him how special the hat was to me and to please not destroy it or chuck it out a window. He promised he wouldn't and I left him with it. Whenever I would see him out after that, I would think of and wonder about my Gator hat. I rarely mentioned it to him, because he continued to be bummed, and the last thing I wanted to do was make him feel worse about himself or bring him even lower in any way. There was a great line spoken by the great Danny Glover in the cute little movie, *Waffle Street*. When the lead character loses his cool with a customer in the diner, Glover's wise old cook guy says, "Why would you tell someone to go to hell when they're already going there?" So, I patiently waited for my hat and eventually it had traded hands with another Georgia fan friend of mine and I occasionally asked for it politely until it came back to me about two and a half years later. I also believe it's safe to say that I have a mutual respect and love for both those Georgia guys.

HINTS 4 HAPPINESS

 JUST BE . . . HAPPY

One of the most significant lessons I have learned is that **HAPPINESS IS A CHOICE!** At a recent time in life, my actual job was working in the kitchen at a restaurant where I used to tend bar. My wage was $13 an hour and I was getting in about 25 hours a week over a four-day period. It was a peaceful, simple job once I acquired the basic skills to cut veggies to spec, marinate chicken wings, whisk up ranch dressing, cook up chili, etc. It paid a bit less than the bartending gig I had had for the last several years. One of the most interesting changes in the job was the reaction from people who were used to seeing me behind the bar, now finding me poking my head from behind the kitchen doors. The owner even said to me, "I don't understand why you would give up bar shifts for this." Another old friend and ex-employer joked, "You're doing it backwards," he said. "Most start in the back of the house and work their way up to the front." Instead of feeling insecure or bad about this state of affairs, I added to his comment by quoting from the great classic movie *Kramer Vs. Kramer* with the amazing Dustin Hoffman and incredibly talented Meryl Streep. When Mr. Kramer, played by Hoffman, was trying to keep custody of his son, he took a lesser-paying job just to be employed so he could battle his ex-wife for the kid. The brutal attorney in divorce court teased how he was climbing down the ladder of success.

LIVING WITH JOY, PEACE, AND HAPPINESS

My realization is how important the actual duties of our job are combined with how we perform it, how much pride we take in it, and ultimately the peace and joy it may give us. Mr. Kramer knew that what made him happiest was being with his son and a lesser job was just fine, making sure that he could attain that goal. This is the same way that I knew the bartending job I was in, though fulfilling and wonderful as it was for two and a half years, was now shrouded in negativity by the powers that be and this little drop in income and prestige or hierarchy was far less crucial to my overall happiness. This awareness and understanding allows me to be grateful, enthusiastic, pleasant and, yes, HAPPY at work every day. As a positive side effect, there are absolutely no regrets about the change.

What we focus our minds on will expand and then create the mood or template for our day. We set this expectation for ourselves each day. Some people start their day by looking for negative things to note and then they convey their pessimistic view to everyone they come across that day. The irony is that they would rather be positive, but they are hedging their bet to prevent disappointment.

I ran into a couple that I know last night. Upon trading pleasantries, as part of her explanation of how she was doing, the woman remarked after an upbeat beginning, "But Thursday the storm is gonna come and that will ruin the next few days." This comment was made on Tuesday afternoon, which was a gorgeous weather day, by the way. My instant thought and then response to her was something like, "Why worry about a weather report that, of course, is pure speculation, and TWO DAYS FROM NOW?" This is the complete and utter opposite of **LIVING IN THE MOMENT!**

HINTS 4 HAPPINESS

Why focus on something so negative and so not important TODAY and NOW, that could easily change many times between now and then? Life is way too short to live this way, yet soooooo many people do. I was also one of those who would drive into work getting myself riled up about something minor that might or might not happen once I got there that may upset me. What a terrible way to prepare yourself for that experience. Don't think how annoyed you would be "if he or she does this, or if so and so comes in." I feel blessed that I have noticed that this is an unfortunate waste of time. Instead, my thoughts while driving to work are more like, "I feel grateful that I woke up today." **MANY DON'T**! Then I remind myself how much I actually enjoy my job, love my coworkers, and respect my boss. I also **LOVE** my community, our town, and the amazing inspiring scenery all around us. I clearly focus on these positives constantly as opposed to looking for some tiny detail of life that's not perfect to marinate in or speak of. This choice has become easier and easier with practice and now I nearly always express positivity to the Universe rather than disappointment.

These bits of information are listed later under the positive lists that I refer to often, but it also feels appropriate to mention here, because they can absolutely increase one's HAPPINESS considerably. Three factors that contribute to HAPPINESS:

1. THE ABILITY TO REFRAME YOUR SITUATION MORE POSITIVELY.

2. THE ABILITY TO EXPERIENCE GRATEFULNESS

3. THE CHOICE TO BE KIND AND GENEROUS

LIVING WITH JOY, PEACE, AND HAPPINESS

 ### TRY FINDING A BALANCE IN ALL AREAS

As I have gotten older and chosen a life as a bachelor, now especially with no living parents, I sometimes find it necessary to parent myself. I think this is a good thing as long as we don't go overboard. The people I generally hang out with, likely because we're in the restaurant business, like to drink a bit. My father, as I mentioned, might be considered by many to have been an alcoholic. I certainly have some of those tendencies through genetics and my experiences growing up. I have gone through phases of drinking a couple of nights a week up to about every night at times. In my inner searching, I have tried to pinpoint exactly why my friends or I feel the need to drink or even be at the bar that often.

What is missing in life that we need that void filled at the bar? I have a few theories that I will discuss throughout, but at this moment I can recall that I was often hoping to meet *that girl*. Recently, it's been more about the plain social interaction that I'm realizing is not necessary either, being that I usually get plenty of that on the job. Looking back at the times when my bar going was tied more to sexual desires, I was buying into what I had been taught by society about needing a romantic partner. I have since discovered that the heartache involved, not to mention the pure stress of searching for, courting, and then keeping even somewhat happy in the process is not something I choose to pursue very often.

The key to achieving **HAPPINESS,** while still getting to experience life fully, is to find that balance. I have watched so many people get caught up in one aspect of life, while neglecting several others. If one part of life

HINTS 4 HAPPINESS

becomes too dominant, then it can be an obsession. This obsession may lead to temporary joy, happiness, or success, but eventually the harm done to the parts of life ignored will surface and often cause far more distress than the little pleasure obtained during the "good time."

One of the lists I used to use, and sometimes still refer to is designed to address this balance in life. I came across a guideline for this exercise in my reading over the years and adopted it on my personal growth journey.

The list goes something like this:

Family
Friends
Exercise
Finance/ Career
Romance
POM
Smiles/ Kindness

LIVING WITH JOY, PEACE, AND HAPPINESS

Then, I would rate each one on a scale of 1 to 10 based on how I felt things were going in each area. I would add up the total numbers and that would give me a total score out of 70 to see where I felt I was at in life. There were times when my scores averaged around 5 to 7 on each. Those total scores were around 35 to 40. If it was much below 40, that expressed almost depression. Then I might jump up to 50-plus and I at least felt I was on the right path. Now my score is consistently between 65 and 70. Balance is GOLDEN.

 TRY THE JOE WALSH RULE

During a great documentary about the rock band, The Eagles, I was deeply impacted by a quote from the music legend, Joe Walsh. He said something like this, "In our lives chaotic events crash into each other causing confusion and we look at our lives and wonder 'what the hell' or question 'why us,' but when we look back at these times, it seems like a finely-crafted novel. The trick is to appreciate the craziness while it's happening."

Since I heard that quote a few years back, I have experienced exactly this state and, thanks to Mr. Walsh, I have often embraced these inexplicable moments and allowed them to be wonderful.

An example happened during a very busy night as I was tending bar at the Italian restaurant. The night before had been fascinating, yet a little stressful, because my fellow bartender and I had gotten scolded by a patron who then threatened to complain to the owner. As much as Jared and I knew the guy was way out of line, we also knew that we could have handled the situation more professionally. So, the next afternoon after going over that uncomfortable scenario in my mind throughout the night before, I was not looking forward to this Friday night shift. I never feel good when I have any sort of conflict with anyone, so I was bothered still as the work night began. As we got into the peak of the dinner rush and my stress level was on the rise, the restaurant's electricity shut off. The lights, the fryers, and the air conditioning all went kaput! Instead of feeling one of those huge stress moments, I just smiled. I knew that the pressure to be perfect was now off. This would be a blackout that we would remember and I figured we might even get off early. My whole demeanor changed and all the stress, pressure, and guilt from the night before melted away. I had a shot with a comrade, rolled up my sleeves, and smiled and laughed through a thoroughly enjoyable and momentous shift. Thank you, Joe Walsh, for your great insight.

These insights often seem simple in theory, but the real tests come during major transitions in life. Previously, I would have called these difficulties when I was less conscious. When I advanced further in understanding, I called them challenges and sometimes I still do. Now, I prefer to call them transitions or maybe just inevitable changes that occur when life becomes too comfortable. Once I chose to inform my boss and very close friend, Angelo, that I would like to request a transfer within the company rather than work with or for two individuals who create an unhappy atmosphere in the restaurant. I slept on the thought to fully grasp the gravity of that decision because I truly did love most of that job and situation. I was deeply bonded with many of my coworkers there. I reveled in my day shift as bartender and I enjoyed pretty much all of my regular customers. Upon further reflection on my choice to tell Angelo I wanted out, I decided I was correct

LIVING WITH JOY, PEACE, AND HAPPINESS

in my decision, based on the tools I had to face the negative atmosphere. Yes, I could have "sucked it up," which was our motto at University of Florida's Pi Lam Fraternity during my junior year when I belatedly decided to join. I just felt that I didn't have the armor to cope with those people who made almost everyone at the restaurant enjoy their job less. As I spent a few days thinking about how I handled things and then went on the job search. I knew that I could have responded better, and I wished I had been more impeccable with my words with one of those people. I kept a very positive attitude throughout this transition, at least on the surface. Deep within me, I had some concerns as to whether I was loyal enough to my boss and good friend. I also wondered if I were foolish and shortsighted by giving up one of the best-fitting work situations I had ever encountered. It struck me during these ruminations, which were tempered by the many Buddhist techniques and tools I had been studying, that these times often spur on the deepest moments of introspection. From these thorough self-examinations, we then form hypotheses that become wisdom in our future dealings and will act as teachings for those we hope to show at some point.

BE A GOOD PERSON, CONTINUOUSLY STRIVING TO BE AN EVEN BETTER ONE AND LEAVE THE UNIVERSE BETTER OFF FOR YOUR HAVING BEEN HERE.

One simple question can best answer whether we are accomplishing this MISSION:

ARE WE HURTING OR CAUSING DISCOMFORT TO ANYONE WITH OUR ACTIONS AND BEHAVIORS…AND ARE WE MAKING THE WORLD A HAPPIER, MORE PEACEFUL AND BETTER PLACE BY

HINTS 4 HAPPINESS

OUR BEING HERE?

 ### TRY BEING NICE LIKE THE "THREE Bs"

I think we all have come across people in our lives who stand out from the rest of us based on pure niceness. I know that I personally have always been intrigued by these individuals. The only downside to knowing these characters is the feeling that many of us less kind people may feel bad about ourselves based on the comparison. Growing up, I knew a few of these types, like my middle school buddy, David Gentille. His parents were very strict Sicilians who required church and goodness from their three sons. David seemed to be kind to everyone. In return, he was loved by all. More recently, in my little mountain town, there were a few people who stood out. John Bunty is appreciated and revered throughout the area for his kindness and upbeat, fun demeanor. I clumped him in with another super nice guy named Jeff, who worked at the local grocery. I thought of them both as a version of Mr. Rogers or the ever-smiling Ned Flanders from *The Simpsons* television show. Then, of course, there was Burton. Burton was one of those people whom everyone loved to be around. He had a beautiful, fun spirit. He worked several different jobs over the years, and, lastly a dishwasher where I was fortunate enough to work as a bartender for a while. Wherever he worked, his purpose and presence were much larger than the job itself. He was always the nonjudgmental, kind, welcoming committee. He had a heartwarming way of making everybody feel special. People often say, "You can't please everyone." In my eyes, Burton proved something that came to mind recently. *WE CAN ALL DO BETTER*. I have yet to come across anyone who didn't like Burton. I have thought to myself

LIVING WITH JOY, PEACE, AND HAPPINESS

whether I could say the same about me. I know there are those who don't care for me, but I also know that since Burton passed away almost two years ago and I have strived to be more like him, there are fewer people out there who would feel negatively about me. I can still do better, and I am **FOREVER** grateful to Burton for showing me what is possible.

If we can only be remembered for one thing, I'll choose KINDNESS. (mOjAf)

There was something else I noticed with the amazing Burton. As I mentioned, he was great at making EVERYONE feel special. He came across in life as giving all individuals many opportunities to show their good sides. Rarely would he actually share with me that he couldn't take a certain person. When he did, he would always preface his statement with, "I have nothing against him (or her)." What was so special about Burton was that he never felt the need to let that person know how much they annoyed him. He simply did not want to hurt their feelings.

One of Burton's best buddies, and now a closer friend of mine with

Burton's passing, confided in me a similar philosophy. Billy seems to like everyone and, from what I have witnessed, greets all with a friendly smile and a tremendous amount of respect. He told me if there are any people in our little community that he doesn't thoroughly appreciate, they likely have no idea that he feels this way. As much as this is the complete opposite of how I used to handle such situations, I now think it is a much more compassionate and admirable way to behave.

Having just left a job, partially due to the management styles of two individuals, I believe the outcome has shown that I have successfully adopted Burt and Billy's method. Both of the people who instigated my change are oblivious to my reasons and seem to hold me in the highest regard. This makes me feel good. Thank you, Billy and Burt!

 TRY FOLLOWING THE GOLDEN RULE

Of course, the Golden Rule states to treat everyone the same way you would like to be treated. I certainly have fallen short in this area too many times to mention, but I do try to live up to this motto. When stressful situations do arise, we tend to forget such principles and our egos take over. If we are not conscious and careful during such duress, we may act like King Kong or Godzilla, stomping everyone in our path to achieve our instant desires. Along with this Golden Rule philosophy, I try to not add any stress, discomfort or suffering to any other individual at any time. This has been one of the leading principles that I have tried to live by my entire life. I'm not sure exactly when or how this concept was introduced to me, but I know that it has stuck with me. It's amazing how quickly we abandon this

LIVING WITH JOY, PEACE, AND HAPPINESS

rule as soon as things don't go exactly the way we want. Our intentions can start off as pure as can be, but when stress occurs, our egos ramp up and we attack a fellow human being, even though it is the exact opposite of how we want to be treated. How do we prevent this from happening? How can we always remember the rule and abide by it consistently? I believe we must make it a huge priority in our lives and then constantly remind ourselves how important it is, just like the journey to happiness. If we make following the GOLDEN RULE as important as our own happiness, then it will actually hasten our goal of such **happiness** with a possible side effect of peace and **joy**. Always remember that we have no idea what others

have been through in life, especially "strangers." I put strangers in quotes because I don't think of anyone as a stranger anymore. My cousin Screech just got back from Bali. He talked of how spiritual, peaceful and beautiful it was there. He also told me how he worked on some things about himself, which is what Bali is known for. When his patience with others was fading because his thirty-plus-hour flight had been a little tiring, he contemplated how long others had flown. This consideration helped him to relax and **accept that we have no idea what difficulties others have endured.** This is exactly the underlying message of the **GOLDEN RULE.**

HINTS 4 HAPPINESS

We all go through the ups and downs of life. We all fail with difficulties of varying degrees. Someone said we all have luggage to carry in life in all different sizes. It's just our journey to carry ours. If we understand this concept, by imagining ourselves in their shoes, then we don't try to add to others' heaviness. I certainly would rather help carry their heaviness then add to it.

 TRY SERVING OTHERS

I don't know if there is any feeling in the world that warms the heart and soul as much as helping others. We fight this desire for so long because our egos have grown too powerful and we have trouble controlling them. We feel we are weak or being taken advantage of for our kindness when, in fact, it makes us grow and feel at peace when we aid others with no real reward in mind for ourselves. It enhances the sense of community and belonging that we all crave deep inside. The many times that I have paid it forward just because it felt like the right thing to do, have led to such profound feelings of happiness that it's still amazing that I don't do more of it. My friend and coworker, Marcos, used the phrase "heart of a servant" to describe many of us who are born into or drawn to the service industry. In the past, I even might have taken offense to that thought, but now I truly appreciate and relate completely with the sentiment. I am proud to serve people in this way and I don't require as much appreciation or thanks anymore, although it is always nice to receive. I have found the reward in the creating an experience for the customer while getting to know them in the process.

LIVING WITH JOY, PEACE, AND HAPPINESS

The Ten Commandments state, of course, to **LOVE thy neighbor.** I recently read a more specific definition of exactly to whom "thy neighbor" refers in this guideline for life. The author says that "thy neighbor" includes anyone around us who needs help that we have the ability to provide. That may seem unrealistic or idealistic, because certain situations occur in which we must use our inner guidance and experience to choose the proper path. We cannot continuously aid those who put themselves in precarious places time after time and don't change this pattern. This point is when we stand back and encourage positive change, yet understand that it is unlikely, and we must observe only with one eye partially closed and hope for the best. There are many more circumstances where we can help someone through a seemingly overwhelming challenge by just showing basic courtesy and kindness, like offering a ride to a stranger or some extra change at a supermarket. When we have less fear and more compassion, we understand that we have all needed this simple gesture before it connects us immeasurably with our fellow humans and the entire Universe.

It bears repeating (and please indulge me my own spin and putting it in super large bold writing):

TREAT EVERYONE WITH THE SAME EXACT AMOUNT OF RESPECT THAT YOU WOULD LIKE THEM TO TREAT YOU AND YOUR ENTIRE FAMILY, INCLUDING YOUR MOTHER OR FATHER, OLD BELOVED GRANDMOTHER OR GRANDFATHER, OR YOUR SON OR DAUGHTER, ETC., and I'll add, under almost any circumstances.

TRY BEING A MENSCH

The loose definition of a *mensch* is one who is kind and generous above and beyond. Probably we have all come across a person like this. It's the epitome of that saying, "He will give you the shirt off his own back." My Nana was like this. My sister Kim describes her as the most loving and kind person she ever knew. This perception of Nana can be corroborated by many others who knew her who are not from a biased family member like Kim and me. Her legal name was Ella, but her nickname was Honey,

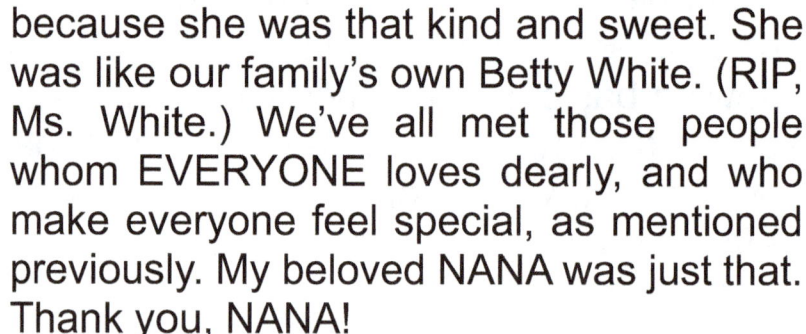

because she was that kind and sweet. She was like our family's own Betty White. (RIP, Ms. White.) We've all met those people whom EVERYONE loves dearly, and who make everyone feel special, as mentioned previously. My beloved NANA was just that. Thank you, NANA!

Having had my share of funerals lately has made me think of my actions on a daily basis and strive to act consistently with how I want to be remembered. I can't expect to be as appreciated, beloved and adored like Nana, Burton, Mr. Rogers, and a few others, but why not aspire to be? This goal gives me great guidance and patience during what I used to think were stressful situations. Also, behaving in a way so that one can even conceive to be remembered in that arena of kindness and appreciation, is in line with my values involving the GOLDEN RULE and to be like JESUS and GOD. How can that lead you astray?

All these examples of people who have inspired us are brought into our lives for that very reason. I now can clearly look back at the many people who have had such a tremendously positive impact on my life. They have all helped encourage me to be a better person. I can only hope and strive to be able to do that every day for others.

TRY MAKING EVERYONE FEEL SPECIAL

The definition of *charisma* that I learned from Tony Robbins is, "To make someone feel good about themselves and you." What a wonderful trait to cultivate! You feel this charisma when you're at one of Tony's seminars. We all have met people who are really charismatic. They are those types who "light up the room" with their presence. My sometime boss and always close friend and "brother" Angelo exudes this quality. He almost always has a giant smile on his face. His enthusiasm for fun and spontaneity is constant and contagious. When I was my less conscious and more uptight self, he often would try to encourage me to lighten up and relax more. He embodies one of the personalities that I wanted to emulate and I feel I have adopted much of his "fun-ness" into my own.

Angelo spreads joy with his charisma. The last few days, I have noticed more and more of how my experiences with people have been very deep, heartfelt, and moving for both parties. This result is partly because I really

HINTS 4 HAPPINESS

do enjoy getting deep with people on a regular basis. I find that most people don't necessarily do so very often. For those individuals, my passion for these conversations can be off-putting or annoying and I have to learn to be more aware. I truly would like everyone to FEEL SPECIAL, or at least BETTER than they felt before seeing me. I am still figuring out how to do that consistently, and part of this effort will be by using my knowledge of psychology and philosophy to decipher the best method of reaching each person. The tricky part, which also may make it the most fascinating, is that everyone is different based on their own experiences. My job is to figure out which angle to use to reach them, connect with them, and then hope they will enjoy the day just a little bit more. In the meantime, I am getting to know them and enjoying that experience in itself. That, I BELIEVE, is what they mean by WIN/WIN! THANK YOU, MY BROTHER ANGELO for teaching me. And hiring me. Again. And again. And again.

(JOURNAL BREAK 1-3-23)
I am adding moments throughout this book when a certain epiphany hits me and to share that experience with you all as it happens. I'm not sure I've ever read a book that ventured to do so, which excites me further. I

must mention two enormously important books to me that departed from normalcy in their style of writing. Be Here Now, *by the incredible, lovely, genius Ram Dass, is printed on brown recyclable paper for one thing. The shape is also very unusual, longer than most and actually makes for easy reading anywhere you may be. It somehow lends itself to being under a tree or on a boat. Also, there are random drawings throughout, spreading his words of wisdom in such a unique way with this combination. He then has his actual story and mini bio in a separate section.*

Matthew McConaughey's thoughtful, deeply honest telling of his amazing story in Greenlights *is peppered with journal pages that he has amassed since he was a child. He uses copies of the actual journals in his handwriting. I thought this was clever, interesting and unique. I will now openly admit that I am borrowing certain novel ideas like this one from those two writers, towards whom I feel incredible respect, admiration and inner love. Thank you, gentlemen, kind spirits, mentors of mine, for all that you have shared with me and the world.*

 ## TRY NOT HURTING <u>ANYONE'S</u> FEELINGS

I let everyone in on the joke. Once I became aware of my destructive behaviors involving being too forthright with my speech, I realized how badly my feelings would be hurt when people spoke ill of me. I began to understand how things I might say even in jest could cause people discomfort later when they rehash the day as I believe most of us do. It became apparent how powerful words can be, whether positive or negative. I made the conscious decision to use my words for good and not bad. It can also go back to the old motherly saying, "If you don't have something **NICE** to say, then don't say anything." I thoroughly agree with this statement now. Usually, the only reason we feel it necessary to tell someone what they did wrong is to quell our own unhappiness or dissatisfaction with our lives. Before I say something negative towards anybody, I try to examine my real intent before saying it. Am I acting purely out of ego? Am I engaging in immature personal semantic "warfare" with someone? Do I really want to hurt their feelings and, if so, why? I now usually choose to add on to their comment about me rather than trying to one up them. This attitude diffuses the little battle and keeps everyone feeling better.

There are many people I have come across over the years who love to engage in this back-and-forth bickering. This behavior also is found in many romantic relationships. Once again, it is a complete waste of time and energy. It is pure EGO at work, and I try constantly not to engage in this. I recently had a "run in" with someone at work, a fellow bartender, who looks for reasons to be unhappy. At this point in our working relationship, he has scolded me many times for borrowing from his bar in the main restaurant, while I work in the same company's more casual sports bar. I have apologized each time, and tried to find common ground, but it's been impossible to appease him. This recent occurrence happened when I wasn't even the culprit of the crime. He laid into me good, saying I was the worst bartender ever and then called me an asshole. I was fairly stunned at the intensity of this particular outburst by him and, though the old me would have gone right back at him, I stood in stunned silence. As he started to walk away, I finally spoke, but it was so lame. I said something like, "You're the biggest jerk in the whole building." Of course, I guess I'd be prouder if I had said nothing at all, but for that moment, I sank to his level.

LIVING WITH JOY, PEACE, AND HAPPINESS

I do feel there has been growth in that I didn't jump right back at him to cause escalation. I am now usually far less compelled to engage in such unconscious behavior.

 ## THE CITY CAN MAKE YOU MEAN

I had this type of combative relationship with many people over the years from acquaintances to coworkers, and even some friends. It's just constant ego bickering, or what we used to call "pissing contests" and I finally understand that nobody wins.

There was one lady who lived in the building I moved into. Her reputation preceded her as an unfriendly, rude person. I think someone even used the B word to describe her. My first and only experience with her confirmed those descriptions of her. She parked behind me, blocking me in because I was unknowingly in her spot. Her choice to block me, rather than just knocking on my door and asking me to move was a perfect example of an unhappy person taking an aggressive stand against a new neighbor and complete stranger, instead of choosing kindness. I wasn't exactly thrilled with her for that choice, when I knocked on her door to ask her to let me out. She pretty much just complained and "bitched" at me the whole walk down. I kept my words and thoughts to myself, I guess I was starting to learn. It's also amazing how seeing a worse or more extreme version of yourself can be so educational. She was a very obviously miserable person who spread that anger and negativity freely. I could relate some, to a lesser degree, but also could openly view what my Cousin Screech calls the **GIANT MIRROR.** Many people had told me to lighten up and slow down before I could have a heart attack. They'd call me **INTENSE.** That's how this angry neighbor lady was, rude, intense, unfriendly, and so uptight. About a month or two later, she died. It was a heart attack. Bless her heart. We also had a guy just like that in the kitchen. He was mad at everyone, always. He was mad at the world. He died, too. If there was a funeral for him, it was nearly empty. So sad. **How do you want to be remembered?**

 TRY TO NOT JUDGE ANYONE

Somewhere along the line in life, we decide we have a right to judge others about EVERYTHING. This is a lousy lesson. It has taken me a lifetime to realize that we are not entitled to anything. Judging is, unfortunately, so common certainly here in America that it could be called a national pastime. From the moment we meet someone, we instantly make opinions about their face, body, hair, clothes, attitude, etc. When we go to a store, a restaurant, or a business of any kind, we immediately sum up what we think of them. We decide whether it's good, bad or somewhere in the middle. Then we think about how we would do things differently or better, because we of course know everything. How did we become experts and criticizers of the Universe?

DOES THIS FUTILE EXERCISE INCREASE OUR JOY, PEACE, OR HAPPINESS? MY ANSWER IS A <u>RESOUNDING NO!</u>

I gradually have been able to shift my focus from judging everything and everybody to just observing and appreciating what I encounter, rather than criticizing and trying to decipher a better way. As I just heard in a Louise

LIVING WITH JOY, PEACE, AND HAPPINESS

Hay YouTube video, "The Universe loves gratitude." I have been much happier observing what I enjoy in experiences and people, rather than what I would change about them. Ram Dass said, **"What you look for everywhere, you will find everywhere."** I use this saying often when I come across chronic complainers, as I certainly used to be. I like to say, "If you look for things to find wrong constantly, you will absolutely find them… and you will never be happy." This is true of pretty much every situation in life. What we focus on expands in our lives. Now that I look for more people who spend their time thinking positively and encouraging others rather than denigrating them, it's amazing how many of these optimists are out there.

In the incredibly powerful movie, based on the book, *The Shack*, there is an amazing scene that deals with judgment. Like any great movie, there are many messages throughout and concepts that provoke thought in the viewers. Each person may be impacted by a different scene based on his or her own experiences. One of my biggest issues and character traits I've worked on improving is my penchant for being too judgmental. When I find that I am falling back into this type of behavior, I will pull up that scene. The beautiful, Godly woman makes a strong point to the character in the movie, explaining vividly that we are not meant to judge. I also refer to the Bible and Jesus who said, "Let he who has not sinned cast the first stone." These things remind me to be more accepting and less judgmental, because none of us is perfect.

HINTS 4 HAPPINESS

 INCLUDE EVERYONE

One thing I've strived to do for many years, as an offshoot from the Golden Rule, is to treat everyone equally and not to leave anyone out. We all know what it feels like to feel isolated and alone among a group of people. It's one of the worst feelings ever. I always watch, for instance, in a bar or restaurant setting when there are more than two people in our party. I try to never have my back to someone and I make sure to make eye contact throughout so everyone feels connected with the situation and the conversation.

I have been fortunate to be part of several social groups over the years that have absolutely given me the sense of belonging that we all crave. These groups were not formal associations, but rather friendship groups that have accepted me as a member. One of those special friendship communities is the one from Florida that I mentioned with Phil and the Key West trip. This group can sometimes include as many as sixty people. When you travel in a pack that big, it can be amazingly fun and you feel indestructible. It's y'all against the world. This attitude can be used in an aggressive, obnoxious way, which I've surely been guilty of over the years, or it can be utilized in a much more loving way. You sometimes can feel the look of envy from others who are either riding solo or in a much smaller group. The compassionate oneness part of me knows that we can touch people in a positive way and include them, so they get to feel a taste of that community love that we do. Everybody desires to feel like they belong. Sometimes we judge so harshly in a moment of time, and it's like we want to hurt that person. Maybe it's a way of getting revenge for the times we felt that way. Whatever causes us to treat others in this way and, in some cases, to not even realize we are doing so, I am well aware that I want NOBODY to feel that left out ever again. If I come across people making someone feel this way in public, I'm usually going to be the one who goes over to console that "outsider" and let him know that **HE OR SHE IS LOVED!**

TRY TO BE LESS DEPENDENT ON OTHERS

Now that I have an increased awareness, which includes the ability to be more objective about my behaviors, both current and past, I can look back on times when I was ridiculously needy. I always felt proud and boasted of being a great friend to people. I was a pretty good friend to some and that became my favorite moniker. What I wasn't completely aware of is what a pain in the butt I could be to those with whom I was tight. Those couple of best friends that I would do anything for had to earn that loyalty by putting up with all of my baggage! These not so admirable traits included my judgment of others, my discomfort in many social situations, rudeness, and impatience, just to name a few. Also, because I judged so many or pushed away others with my brash and brutal honesty, the few that were left in my circle had to carry my full weight when I did need someone for any reason. If that friend wasn't there for me to the level that I felt I would be for them, then there was some kind of retribution in my attitude, much like two- to five-year-old children might act if they don't get their way.

It's incredible to me that it took fifty years for me to recognize how silly this behavior is and how much pain and wasted emotion was exhausted over all those years. Now I'm amazed by how common these types of tactics

HINTS 4 HAPPINESS

are in people of all ages around us. The guilt trips, silent treatments, angry reactions and passive aggressive pissing contests that occur everywhere daily create negativity and divisiveness. I have made the conscious decision to not get caught up in these traps again. I don't NEED any particular person anymore. I do believe that we are social beings and we do get comfort from other beings around us. I enjoy human interaction and contact with others and do find it useful, enjoyable and special in bonding with many. The difference now is that I don't depend on one or two people to ALWAYS be there for me. I have discovered how exhausting that can be for the other person and I don't want to create such suffering for anyone, let alone my closest buddies.

As I have become far less needy, I still understand the strength, comfort and joy that is experienced from the deep relationships we have with others. I

enjoy my alone time so much more than I used to, but there is sometimes a challenge of how to properly balance this with social interaction. Now that my friendship horizons have expanded because I judge less and have removed most of my abrasive tendencies, there seem to be endless opportunities to connect with others. Because I'm not getting all my personal interaction and companionship from one or two people, it is much less stressful for them. This only strengthens the bond with others because they don't feel taxed upon when we spend time together. In fact, I strive for them to always feel better having spent time with me.

LIVING WITH JOY, PEACE, AND HAPPINESS

 GETTING BUTT HURT

This term is one of my favorite southern sayings that I have picked up living in North Carolina. Being **BUTT HURT** describes a situation where people get upset or offended by something that someone else says or does. Anthony Robbins used to like to say "peeved" instead of angry to downplay the emotion of the moment. I like to use **butt hurt** in the same way. Once we realize that nothing should really offend us or bother us in what others say, it becomes much easier to let these little things go, rather than stress over them.

◆ LET IT BE

When I first moved to the mountains, I found very few other Jewish individuals up here. Occasionally, one of the locals would say something like, "I didn't mean to jew ya down." I even had a boss that I really liked who once said to me, "We had to leave Boca, 'cause it was too ethnic." I thought, "Boca? Ethnic?" Then he followed up with, "Too many Jews." He didn't know at that point that he was talking to a Jew. My heart sank that day. I eventually came to realize that his comment and feelings towards the Boca Jews really had nothing to do with me.

I have since striven to follow the Second Agreement from ancient Toltec wisdom, **TAKE NOTHING PERSONALLY**. As difficult as this is to follow, just making the effort has helped me be happier and not worry as much about what others think, when I know that I am acting properly and in line with my mission and values. It is amazing the change that occurred in my life when I began not getting **BUTT HURT anymore.** Coupled with taking nothing personally, my happiness and joy increased almost immeasurably. So many people I come in contact with daily live the opposite way, much like I did before. I witness their interpretations of others' actions. The stress, anger, resentment and overall misery that people put themselves through because **THEY FEEL** they have been wronged is astronomical. These emotions and negative feelings are all based on assumptions and useless internal dialogue. They eat us up inside. I have trained my mind to do so little of this that it's basically nonexistent. This practice has helped to create the joyous, peaceful, adventurous and love-filled life that I am blessed to be enjoying.

LIVING WITH JOY, PEACE, AND HAPPINESS

THE FOUR AGREEMENTS:

1. BE IMPECCABLE WITH YOUR WORDS
2. TAKE NOTHING PERSONALLY
3. MAKE NO ASSUMPTIONS
4. ALWAYS DO YOUR BEST

I had a few situations arise as I was trying to be a nicer, more patient and overall better person. People tried to test me, push me, fight me and just plain take advantage of my newfound kindness. This can be a real challenge. How can you be kind, compassionate, and generous when people abuse that privilege and you can't really afford to give it? I found that courage is probably the best answer. It is easier said than done, but I have been able to summon the courage and strength to say no, while staying kind and compassionate.

 TRY LEARNING EVERY DAY

Study => Learning => Knowledge = WISDOM

As Tony Robbins taught me in his books and seminars years ago, the tools and methods are out there in abundance if we only look and utilize them. I use many of these techniques to raise my positive energy daily. They act as consistent motivation and affirmation of the person I want to be and represent on a normal basis. When I find myself bored with down time or I feel my energy or POM is slightly lacking momentarily, I use the many lists,

HINTS 4 HAPPINESS

techniques, or methods to raise my enthusiasm and energy level back up to where I like it to be. There was a time, a few years back, when I got so distracted with achieving financial and career goals that I lost the lust for learning. This seems to happen to many people at some point on their journey. Also, we tend to get to a point based on whatever achievements we have amassed, to feel like we know so much that we want to just talk, talk, talk about ourselves and what we think we know. We forget that we can learn SOMETHING from absolutely ANYONE and EVERYONE if we only close our mouths and LISTEN. If we stop trying to compete with or one up the other person with OUR story and truly pay attention to theirs, then we open ourselves up to endless possibilities and wisdom. I also like to recite and affirm other words of wisdom from those who have lived before us.

Tony also taught me his awesome acronym, **CANI**, that has to do with continuing to learn:

C onstant
A nd
N ever-ending
I mprovement

I liked this concept so much that I also use CANI to describe the bracelets that I wear on my left hand. They came about with the passing of Burton, our town's beloved angel. The bracelets remind me constantly to judge less and to continue to work on being a better person. CANI is spiritual! Those of us who are "Spiritual Seekers," as some call us, are aware of how important CANI is on our journey.

LIVING WITH JOY, PEACE, AND HAPPINESS

 ### TRY TAKING CARE OF YOURSELF FIRST

This concept is a little tricky to explain properly. The compassionate one in me may first think this sounds selfish. The opposite is actually true if we understand that we cannot serve others or God if we are not in a good place ourselves. This is true of our physical well-being in addition to our mental, spiritual and emotional health. When I went through some extremely difficult times in my journey and found myself depressed, lonely, frustrated, angry and sad, I exhibited those pains externally by lashing out at anyone in my path. This way, I believe, is how most people handle their stress. We act out, yell, and blame other people, most often the ones closest to us who are caring about us and trying to help us the most. How foolish, irrational, and ungrateful is this? Looking back with clearer vision, I see how I reacted and can now recognize such behavior in others. Buddhism has taught me through its own definition, TO FIND AND ELIMINATE THE SUFFERING IN ONE'S LIFE.

I have been fortunate enough through God's help to achieve a pretty high level of joy because of the elimination of most, if not all, suffering. This has come from and will continually grow from my focus, which inspires me to practice, study, and meditate on this philosophy. Immediately following my commitment to ease my own suffering or stress in life is my resolution not to add to anyone else's stress or suffering. Furthermore, I am now fully aware that if I am struggling internally or physically, it becomes much more difficult to be conscious of others' care, feelings, and needs. My sincere hope is to be able to also encourage all those around me to find peace and joy in their lives, which I can best excel in if I'm at my absolute best.

HINTS 4 HAPPINESS

I like to use an analogy with the way the airlines explain how to use your oxygen masks in case of an accident. They say for you to put on your own mask before helping others. Our own personal wellness is the same way. We must be good first before we can truly be our highest selves and in turn serve others best.

 TRY NOT BEING A BURDEN TO ANYONE

Once our own suffering is eliminated, our mission is to also cause no suffering to other sentient beings. For this reason, we avoid eating animals in our diet as much as possible. I try not to cause pain or discomfort to other creatures of any kind. Aren't we all God's creations? So, who am I to treat any of these beings with anything but LOVE? If we are failing in this area and not advancing our growth, then we are not trying hard enough. I have recently noticed the pattern in certain people to duplicate certain unproductive or even destructive behaviors that keep them in a never-ending cycle of misery. These people continue to blame others for all their problems, rather than put in the REAL WORK to create change from within. They then espouse their frustrations to the world again and again while adding to their own irrational misery. It came to my attention that these sufferers should **LIVUROBIT!**

I have read somewhere over the years about this exercise where you make up and write your own obituary as if you have died. This may include the physical and financial achievements you hope to attain, but for me it would focus more on the overall person I want to become. Then once it is written, I would view it often as a mission statement and guideline on how to act,

LIVING WITH JOY, PEACE, AND HAPPINESS

interact, and live each day. For example, here is what mine looks like:

mOjAf DIED AT 90 YEARS OF AGE, WHILE FEEDING THE DUCKS AT HIS BELOVED MILL POND IN FRONT OF THE WATERFALL IN THE LITTLE MOUNTAIN TOWN THAT WAS HIS HOME FOR THE LAST FORTY YEARS.

Nobody's obituary tells the truth of how they are truly remembered. It doesn't speak of the whispers that are said about people who were not very nice, kind of an asshole, selfish as shit, a pain in the ass, or many, many complaints about the way they treated others, etc.

These are traits we know about ourselves that we pretend don't exist or we lessen our fault in them. Our ego is great at coming up with excuses for our actions. When I sit through these funerals that come my way, it reconfirms the fact that I want to be remembered for good things. I want to be known for leaving everything and everyone better off for my having been here, PERIOD! So, I know

that this takes priority over ego or anything else. I just have to always keep that near the forefront of my psyche, so that I am living congruently with my purpose and values on a daily basis. Tricky work at times, but it's so important to me that it's absolutely worth it to put in the effort. This is our legacy and our presentation to God.

 BLAME ONLY CAUSES PAIN

I described earlier how certain people live in negativity and dwell in this misery. I believe the major cause of their problems is their constant focus on blaming others. At the root of this blame is people's inability to take complete responsibility for their lives. This trait seems to be a societal thing that has become customary, especially in challenging times like the current Covid pandemic, where you see people judging every action by everyone else. Doing so has caused violence, stress, hatred, and an overall feeling of separateness. I have noticed this behavior at my jobs. When something goes wrong in any way, the first question people tend to ask is, "Who did it" or "Whose responsibility was it?" Our "learned" instinct seems to be, who's at fault. We look for peace or solace in these situations by pointing out the culprit, which relieves us of blame and we think we'll feel better about things. The truth is that it then creates anger, frustration, and narcissistic feelings that we are **BETTER** than **THEY ARE.** People who are unaware that their frustrations are from within and not from other people's actions continue to live in the cycle of negativity. Some of us are fortunate enough to gain clarity in knowing that we can, in fact, decide to create our own peace and happiness by being accountable for our lives, our emotions, and our attitude toward everything that happens to us. A huge part of accomplishing

LIVING WITH JOY, PEACE, AND HAPPINESS

this lofty goal is to constantly remind ourselves how fortunate we are and how grateful we should be for the many blessings with which we have all been gifted. If you ever doubt this, just lookup what life is like in less wealthy countries than ours or imagine the real difficulties our ancestors faced accomplishing simple tasks like taking a shower back in the day. We take so many of these things for granted daily. If we focus more on these ideas and less on what we think other people should or should have done, we would all be happier and more at **PEACE** with **OURSELVES.**

LISTS THAT HELP US GROW AND LEARN:

OPTIMISTS CREED

1. Be so strong that nothing can disturb my peace of mind.
2. Make all friends feel there is something of value in them.
3. Talk health, happiness and prosperity to everyone I meet.
4. Look at the sunny side of everything and make my optimism come true.
5. Wear a cheerful countenance at all times and greet every living creature with a smile.
6. Think only the best, work only for the best, and expect the best.
7. Be as enthusiastic at the success of others as I am of my own.
8. Forget mistakes of the past and press on to greater achievements of the future.

HINTS 4 HAPPINESS

9. Spend so much time on the improvement of myself that I have no time to criticize others.

10. Be too large for worry, too noble for anger, too strong for fear, and too happy to permit the presence of trouble.

PATIENCE IS NOT ONLY A VIRTUE, BUT A TRUE MEASURE OF CHARACTER. - mOjAf

10 LAWS OF DHARMA

1. PATIENCE
2. FORGIVENESS
3. DEITY OR SELF-CONTROL
4. HONESTY - Being fair in all dealing
5. SANCTITY - Clean body and mind
6. CONTROL OF ONE'S SENSES
7. REASON
8. TRUTHFULNESS
9. KNOWLEDGE AND LEARNING
10. LOSS OF ALL ANGER

LIVING WITH JOY, PEACE, AND HAPPINESS

8 PILLARS OF JOY

Of the heart:
1. Forgiveness
2. Gratitude
3. Compassion
4. Generosity

Of the mind:
5. Perspective
6. Humor
7. Humility
8. Acceptance

3 FACTORS THAT MOST INFLUENCE OUR HAPPINESS:

1. The ability to reframe our situation more positively. (Become a master at finding a silver lining in any circumstances.)

2. The ability to experience gratitude. (This can be accomplished daily, hourly, eventually momentarily.)

3. The choice to be kind and generous. (None of us is perfect but if our intention is pure and we consciously attempt to live these qualities, we will come remarkably close.)

HINTS 4 HAPPINESS

DAILY REMINDERS

1. Enjoy the day
2. Be here now
3. Be nice, like the 3 B's
4. Be the Buddha
5. Just be

CONNECT WITH THE UNIVERSE AND LEAVE IT BETTER FOR YOUR HAVING BEEN THERE

TREAT ALL BEINGS WITH RESPECT

The ultimate guide for this concept is of course the GOLDEN RULE – *DO UNTO OTHERS AS YOU WOULD HAVE DONE TO YOU.* This rule is at the basis of my desire to be kind to others. It runs through my mind constantly, throughout every day. I'm very glad that it does. I'm not completely sure where I first heard it or when it became cemented into my brain, but it definitely has. I certainly have not always embodied the rule perfectly, but I definitely strive to do so. With my recent awareness it has become easier and more ingrained to follow through with this principle in ALL of my interactions with others.

Being back in the restaurant business for the last fifteen years has served as a constant reminder to treat everyone with a tremendous amount of respect NO MATTER WHAT! For some reason, many people feel it is okay to scold, berate, or yell at strangers if their meal is not exactly what they ordered and out to them fast. This behavior happens in many businesses of course, but seems to run rampant in our industry. I have been guilty of this in the past when I was less conscious and less focused on being a better person and connecting more beautifully with the universe. Now, when I witness others behaving this way, whether towards me, my coworkers, or other poor souls who are doing their best to serve the public, I no longer take it personally. I will do my best to console the abused party and will try to softly encourage the unconscious party to lighten up and focus on the positive. Often, I actually feel bad for the offender because they are obviously unhappy with their own existence if they get that upset over an over-cooked burger.

LIFE IS VERY SHORT THERE IS NO TIME FOR FUSSING AND FIGHTING, MY FRIENDS!

◆ APPRECIATING NATURE

If we look at the intricacy of all God's creatures, from ants to millipedes to birds to squirrels and butterflies to the amazing gorgeous flowers, it's hard not to believe in miracles. As a young child, I felt this incredible connection with animals large and small. I think many kids feel this way, yet somewhere along the line in life we lose this bond. We get caught up in "making a living" and chasing dreams, etc., and then these creatures become nuisances and in our way.

HINTS 4 HAPPINESS

I clearly remember when I was a child under eight years of age in New Jersey hanging out in my backyard on my swing set. There would always be one fly hanging around. Of course, most flies look pretty similar, so it's fairly doubtful that I was ever seeing the same one. But to my young, childish, imaginative open-minded brain, I felt sure enough that he was my friend to name him. Sammy, I think, was the name I chose. Years later, in my young adult years, I thought of ants in this loving way. I thought about how thoughtless many people can be while purposely stepping on ants or other critters. It occurred to me that these frantic ants are up to something with all that running around. They also carry crumbs and things and seem organized in their long lines along the cracks of the pavement. They also seem to communicate with each other in their craziness. I wondered what could be going on in little Andy Ant's life when humans might carelessly stomp out his existence. Maybe he was graduating to a higher level or getting married that day, but we callously crushed him. Maybe we affected many ant lives negatively with our ignorance. This may seem silly or over the top, but who's to say what's happening with them? I just know that I would rather consider the possibilities and make an effort to affect all creatures positively and not negatively wherever I can.

Now that I'm in my 50s, I have started naming many animals again, from the many ducks and geese at our beloved duck pond, to the neighborhood bull and the horse on the corner. I just have this overall appreciation for all of these beings. The gorgeous chatty birds of all kinds, the chaotic squirrels and chipmunks that I try to avoid with my car, to the magical deer, otters and bears that come across my path in the mountains. If I can do one little thing to improve their experience on earth, why wouldn't I?

LIVING WITH JOY, PEACE, AND HAPPINESS

 ## CHILDLIKE WONDER

When we learn to slow down and appreciate things like we used to, our eyes open up wide again. We see details that we haven't noticed since we were children. I now look at leaves, rocks, even cracks in roads or trees that now exhibit figures or shapes that fascinate me. In my prep cook job, one of my favorite tasks is cutting green peppers because the shapes are so unique that it's reminiscent of Forrest Gump's line about a box of chocolates. "You never know what you're gonna get." One day, I sliced a pepper and the core had a perfect smiley face in it. I showed everyone at work and even took pictures of it to send to friends and family. It felt like God was trying to make me smile, so why not share that with others? Whether these little signs are messages or so-called coincidences, which I clearly have made up my mind about, they certainly keep life more interesting.

HINTS 4 HAPPINESS

They are **UNIVERSAL CONFIRMATIONS (UC)** for me and if that adds to my eccentricity to others, I'm completely comfortable with that perception as well. I believe that these "silly" observations assist me in getting the most out of this human experience. I started to notice these UCs being especially abundant over the last few years. I now consider these UCs to be little clues to the ongoing mystery of life. Like John Denver says in his song, "Thank God I'm a country boy!" and "Life ain't nothin' but a funny, funny riddle…" These clues are hints to many answers that we seek in life. I choose to note them along the journey and find they may not make total sense when they first appear, but if we are aware and paying attention, the message will eventually become clear.

LIVING WITH JOY, PEACE, AND HAPPINESS

MY DEFINITION OF A UNIVERSAL CONFIRMATION IS:

That experience that feels like a coincidence, also known as SYNCHRONICITY, where something occurs after you thought of a certain person, song, movie or happening that then resurfaces soon after no real explanation of how or why this "premonition" materialized.

This reconnection with my inner child has created such an amazing level of joy even when I'm involved in menial tasks, like in the case of the green peppers. Sadghuru likes to say, "If you are bored, then you aren't very good company, are you?" Often, in the restaurant business, we can have some very quiet or down times. The young people I work with love to complain about being bored. I then throw that Sadghuru line at them. I do understand what they mean, because I used to feel similarly. Now, living in the moment and having become more like my four- or five-year-old self than my fifty-four-year-old self, I rarely feel the slightest bit under stimulated. I can easily be amused or entertained by watching the clouds or any other myriad of things happening out the window. Currently, there is a gang of homeless cats that live underneath

the restaurant next door to the one at which I work. The manager lady and I have taken it upon ourselves to make sure these cats are well fed. In return for such consideration, we have gotten to have a special relationship with these adorable creatures. We often talk about the pure joy they have brought to our workday like when they excitedly respond to our greeting by jumping out of the bushes and running to us. Watching them excitedly shove their tiny noses into the cat food can and then look up with dirty faces like a two-year-old eating ice cream is heartwarming and priceless. On a slow day at work I can spend a good part of the day watching these kittens wrestle around and play with branches. I choose this activity rather than joining the less conscious folks who end up in constant gossip or other negative criticisms of everyone and everything they dislike about work.

ASK THE UNIVERSE FOR HELP OR WHAT YOU NEED

When I was coming out of one of the most difficult periods of my life a few years back, I was close to giving up hope. My desire was to be happier and I was closing in on what was preventing most of my peace and joy. I realized that I wasn't happy with the way I was treating others. I had just gotten back to my beloved little mountain town from my journey in which I had moved apartments eight times in two and a half years. I had stumbled through job after job with major frustration in not finding the right fit. Like Dorothy trying to get back to Kansas, I knew more and more that I just wanted to be HOME! I was starting to understand that WHAT I was doing for work was far less important than WHERE I was and WHO I was with. I told myself that being back up in the mountains in the most comfortable place

LIVING WITH JOY, PEACE, AND HAPPINESS

with the special neighbors and friends that I loved dearly and who accepted me with my many faults was the most IMPORTANT thing. I decided, upon coming back, that I would never take these things for granted again. I was feeling mostly good about life being back here, but at work I still was getting upset by little comments by customers or unfulfilled coworkers. I was still chippy towards some or engaging in childish pissing contests with others in the heat of the work battle, which usually meant the restaurant rush times when we lost our manners with each other. I remember being disappointed in myself for failing at overcoming those moments to the point where I looked up at the ceiling and spoke to God for one of the first times. I said, "God, you see I'm trying, BUT look at what I'm dealing with." Basically, I was saying, "throw me a friggin' bone here..." to quote the great Mike Myers in *Austin Powers*. About the same time, I had written down a line I came up with that went something like this, **"IF CONTINUED SELF-IMPROVEMENT IS, IN FACT, A FALLACY AS I'M STARTING TO BELIEVE, IF THERE IS A HEAVEN, AT LEAST GOD OR SOMEONE SHOULD SEE THAT I KEEP TRYING!"**

With the help of Ram Dass's *Be Here Now*, and many other factors, which include, in my opinion, my finally letting **God in...**I found PEACE and the strength to overcome these judgments of others. The tenth principle of the Ten Laws Of Dharma took hold and I had a complete **LOSS OF ANGER.** This concept still needed to be "watered" and cultivated, but the seed had started to grow in me and now it is a huge part of the foundation for my peace, joy, and contentment.

HINTS 4 HAPPINESS

UNDERSTANDING THAT WE'RE ALL CONNECTED

When we are young children, especially before about four years old, we seem to have an instant bond with other people. This bonding can be seen at any playground across the Universe. Toddlers are trusting of other children and adults. It is not until our parents and teachers teach us to BEWARE OF STRANGERS, that we start to look at others as enemies or competitors rather than compatriots. It's a shame that it has become the norm to distrust others or try to beat and even destroy them. **US AGAINST THEM** is the theme. I, too, fell into this way of thinking for the last forty-plus years until realized we are wasting time and missing out on so much by pushing people away rather than connecting with them. I always found it interesting that, when we travel to other parts of the country or the world, we can instantly bond with someone from our home country, state or hometown. If you live in New York City and you're on vacation in Texas, on a plane maybe, you're going to instantly feel attached to your fellow New Yorker. However, when you're back home in Queens, you'll step on that guy to grab a cab or get the last subway seat. Also, while driving anywhere, it's amazing how we speed up to not allow someone to merge into our lane or come out from a stop sign. WE ACTUALLY SPEED UP! What is our real hope by doing that? Do we want to make them crash and, God forbid, get hurt or even DIE? Hopefully we're not that hateful, but just distracted by our competitiveness and selfishness that we MUST GO FIRST!

I had a situation when I was in college that ultimately taught me this lesson. I was driving home from the University of Florida (GO GATORS) over the

LIVING WITH JOY, PEACE, AND HAPPINESS

holiday break, as we all commonly did, when a car loaded up with clothes and things moved into my lane on the highway. I laid on the horn abruptly to keep the car from running into mine. The driver corrected quickly, but must have hit the dirt shoulder, which then caused her vehicle to flip over right beside me. I was scared as heck that the passengers would be injured. I stopped and ran over to check on them. It turns out that the two girls inside were just fine, thank God. Their windows had been open, so they were both covered in the same dirt that caused the wreck. They were FSU girls from my college rival Free Shoes University, so once I knew they weren't hurt, I did enjoy a little snicker that they got kind of dirty. The police came and saw how limited their visibility was because of all the crap they stuffed in their car, so he knew I wasn't at fault and sent me on my way. Looking back at that incident, I am first and foremost so grateful that nobody got hurt. Secondly, I view that moment as a very important lesson in being more courteous on the road. I have pondered as to whether I needed to have beeped the horn so voraciously, even though everything worked out okay. So, I can only imagine how horrible I would have felt if my haste, impatience, or anger ever caused somebody to get injured. That's why I happily wave people on if I'm holding them up, or if they are trying to get in. Please, y'all, go right ahead. I'm in no hurry. The South, the mountains, the people, and **GOD** have taught me to **SLOW DOWN AND BE NICE!** The bonus side effect to their amazing advice was and is **HAPPINESS!**

I NOW choose to be conscious and try not to prevent some car from merging or trying to just get in. Once we realize that we can find common ground with every other human, we then feel the true connection with every being in the UNIVERSE.

HINTS 4 HAPPINESS

 ## WE ARE ALL IN THIS TOGETHER

Do you want to make a positive or negative impact on the world? I think of this question when it comes to those who choose to litter. One of my older friends taught me this years ago when I thought I was being cool, throwing an empty can out of a car window. My friend Brett so eloquently stated, "That ain't right." And he **WAS RIGHT!** I don't litter anymore, in fact I pick up trash whenever possible if I see it out and about. Do you leave things better or worse for your having been here? I try to act that way each and every day. In addition to spreading physical trash with litter, some people as mentioned earlier will put garbage out into the Universe with their negativity, polluting the air with pessimism. Do you want to be known for that or be able to rest easy that you have left a scent of fun, joy, roses or cookies, rather than sewage. I know how I'd rather be remembered. Sadghuru says there are just two ways to live. Either people are joyful that you're here or they are joyful when you're gone. What is your choice?

Do you need a crowd to have a good time? Random connections with one or two people in a strange town can be magical. In society, certainly in my experience in America, we learn that being with other people makes us "cool." Being alone in public has been thought to be sad or a sign of having no friends, which back in high school times would brand you a loser. There was a stigma attached to that, especially on a Friday or Saturday night, which were known to be date nights or, at the very least, a time to be with friends. I remember that in my teen years up to probably my thirties, I would have been embarrassed to be at a bar, restaurant, or especially a movie by myself. Looking back, I realize how limiting that

LIVING WITH JOY, PEACE, AND HAPPINESS

was to my leisure life. Now, I embrace the freedom and comfort of going where I want, when I want, without the restraint of needing someone else with me. Some people are so trained to go to places that are popular that they are instantly disappointed if the place they're at is not hopping. I often find this situation at restaurants where I work. They disappointedly say, "I thought you'd be more crowded." Instead of appreciating that we're able to provide excellent service because it's quieter and even get to speak with the customer rather than running endlessly, they focus on what's not there – more people. These are the types who would also be complaining if it were too crowded to give them great service that they demand. They are guaranteeing themselves disappointing results instead of enjoying the moment and making the best of every situation.

HINTS 4 HAPPINESS

As for traffic, a boiling point for unhappy people, my perspective has changed dramatically. I let cars in front of me merge or change lanes **WHENEVER** possible, which is almost always. Since that incident with those girls in college where they could have been seriously injured, I know that I would rather let them all in. They are not against me or keeping me from anything. We get there when we get there, and I'm just fine with that. Everyone is a part of the **UNIVERSE**! **WE ARE SO CONNECTED AND IN IT TOGETHER.** If only more people could understand this! Wow! We would be a much happier, more peaceful, kind, and joyous community of humans. **JUST IMAGINE…** To quote the late, great John Lennon, *"You may call me a dreamer, but I'm not the only one."*

 FINDING JOY IN THE JOY OF OTHERS, EVEN STRANGERS

There is a German word ***schadenfreude,*** which basically means to get enjoyment from the misery of others. I have a friend who openly admitted feeling this way. I called him out on it because I sensed the glee he derived from others' and my hard luck situations. I was very sad for him. For someone to like the struggles of those closest to him, rather than root for their HAPPINESS, is no way to live. I believe that this attitude comes from a deep-seated feeling of lack and frustration with one's own life. In his case, it was based on loneliness and desire to find a life partner. Since he found his soulmate, I'm pretty sure he doesn't suffer *schadenfreude* anymore, GOD BLESS.

There are many people out in the world, like me, who live with the opposite philosophy. I have rediscovered the ability to feel PURE JOY, while just

LIVING WITH JOY, PEACE, AND HAPPINESS

witnessing others experience such deep happiness. We all had this trait as children. We could watch other kids on a swing set or pony ride and FEEL their excitement. Then as adults we get so caught up in our daily tasks and tedious missions that we don't allow time for such **CHILDISHNESS.** I have realized that part of making this journey of life so beautiful and **MAGICAL** is slowing down to notice, appreciate, and maybe even **MARINATE IN IT**!

Today, for example, I had several moments like this, from watching our stray, semi-adopted restaurant cats devour the food we brought them, to watching a family of out-of-towners frolic in the snow together, to a group of friends warmly reuniting at lunch. Rather than be annoyed by a large group that didn't really affect my day much like the old me would, I got to observe and enjoy the dynamics of this fun group! **Perspective** is **AMAZING!**

In the Optimist Club Creed, which I have listed previously, there is that one line that says, "Be as enthusiastic about the success of others as I am of my own." This idea is a beautiful concept. I am proud to say that I embrace this quote often. If a friend lets you in on good news of something in his life, do you feel HAPPINESS for him? Or do you fall for the "Veruca Syndrome?" For example, let's say a friend tells you that he or she won a trip to Hawaii. Do you feel that joy or do you think, "I need a vacation," or "I never win anything"? It's amazing how many people respond in these ways rather than being HAPPY for a friend. It's the self-centeredness that we have learned as a society, a ME-FIRST ATTITUDE.

125

FEEDING DUCKS, SQUIRRELS ET AL

I have had this amazing bond with animals since my early youth, as I described with my fly and ant friends. Now that I have reconnected with nature, I have begun to remember how good interacting with these many different animals in their world makes me feel. There is something so grounding and connecting when you give in this way. The feeling I get when the ducks run across the field to me because they recognize me and know food is coming is heartwarming. Watching the squirrels grab nuts that I throw them and stash them in their little jaws makes me smile every time. Their little hands and the way they use them fascinates me endlessly. Chipmunks, too. These interactions connect me with my neighborhood, community, and, yes, the Universe. I heard someone describe the medication of nature and how it soothes us. This is a perfect way of putting it. When I feel life is a little too hectic or I need to get out some frustration, nature eases it all if we can just **LET IT IN.**

 ## FRIENDSHIP

Where to start here is tricky. Many times, I have felt like this is the most natural thing for me, to be a friend. I have prided myself on being a great friend since I was very young. I also realized early on how important friends were to me. It seemed crucial to me to have one very special "best" friend. As I look back over the years from childhood until just a few years back, there always was one person on whom I could expect to depend. That person

LIVING WITH JOY, PEACE, AND HAPPINESS

also had my almost undying loyalty. I specifically said "almost" because, upon thorough reflection, I now realize that my friendship was definitely far too conditional. I used to put so much pressure on that "best friend" that it was too much for many to handle. If they let me down, I would give them hell with silent treatments or other childish, passive aggressiveness. It took one of my more recent close friends to express to me how unfair and needy my behavior and pressure could be. I hope that I have ultimately become a better friend. I also have learned to not pile that responsibility on any one individual. Part of the reason I ended up with one close friend was that I could be such a complaining pain in the butt, that, as one good friend said to me, "I LOVE YOU MAN, BUT ONLY A FEW PEOPLE CAN TAKE YOU!"

I was just becoming objective enough to hear those words. I asked my friend to repeat what he said. He started to apologize and backtrack. I explained that I wasn't upset or hurt, but I appreciated what he said. I knew that I did NOT want to be that guy. I had to change.

Now, after talking of the pitfalls and mistakes I made with friendship, let's get to the incredible, amazing, fulfilling, and magical times with friends and how absolutely rewarding the experiences CAN be.

Even those of us who feel like the biggest losers or the absolute nobodies, as long as we have that one buddy, it will be all right. That is the amazing POWER OF FRIENDSHIP. I have considered myself a "friend guy" ever since I can remember. Whatever difficulty you go through, from the death of a loved one, a breakup with a girlfriend or boyfriend, wife, husband to getting fired from a job, a good friend can make it bearable.

HINTS 4 HAPPINESS

On the even more positive side, the MOMENTS in life, which I speak of often, are in many cases created with those friends whom we love dearly. Simple moments can become unforgettable treasures just because you're hanging with such amazing, dear friends. One of my favorite ways to spread HAPPINESS among my friends is to send them pictures of us having good times on vacation, parties, or other special gatherings. I believe these reminders of momentous, happy times can snap people out of the doldrums of daily tasks, even for just a MOMENT, to add a piece of JOY to their day.

Another priceless thing about friends is the ability to share our victories with them. We all have these moments in life that are little steps towards our growth. They are milestones, from first kisses or fights, to graduations, promotions, or other hard-earned achievements. The feeling of reaching that goal is incredible and maybe it's only matched by sharing that news with your **BEST FRIEND!**

For me, that best friend changed throughout the years. The one who was steadily there to cheer on my good times and nurse me through the bad, in addition to the BEST TIMES of the year was:

(DRUM ROLL, PLEASE!)

MY MOM!

LIVING WITH JOY, PEACE, AND HAPPINESS

Mom was always the first or second phone call I made when I experienced good or bad news.

Now, I would like to look back on, and kindly and sincerely thank those many friends along the way whom I considered to be my BEST friend at some point in time. I'm going to try to list accurately all of them. Also let me apologize to you all for my being a needy mess at times. Thank you for most likely being a *Bridge Over Troubled Waters* for me during tough times. Thank you, Simon and Garfunkel for that song and others to help me through good and bad times. I would like to encourage y'all to remember some of your PRICELESS, SUPERSTAR friends along the way in life who were there for you, maybe even make a list too.

So, here goes:

In New Jersey from 1970-1976, there was Richard Schneider. Thank you for being my buddy with whom to explore the woods. I remember our being together a lot. Also, there was Susie Levant. Thank you for being the first of many cool, competitive chicks with whom I loved to hang out, ride bikes together, wrestle around with, and to whom I was also attracted.

Then in Sarasota, on Bird Key, there was Roy. He was my bestie until we

got in a fight over who knows what. He gave me a left hook before I knew anything and my ears rang. I'm pretty sure I ran the block home. Thanks, Roy, for giving me my first beating. I deserved it, I'm sure.

There was Andre Spencer, my first close African American friend, who slept over when the only black folks on Bird Key were the help. I appreciate my parents for not caving in to social limitations.

Then, one of my oldest, BEST FRIENDS to this day, is MAGDI. There have been so many great times, memories, and milestones with this LIFELONG PAL. He knew and found GOD way before I did and was quietly showing me how to be kinder, more compassionate, and overall a better person. Love you, my friend.

LIVING WITH JOY, PEACE, AND HAPPINESS

Thank you, Christian and Shannon, too.

Then to South Florida where there was Juan, aka Chichi. We were buddies, chasing girls, hanging out in the villas with Mike and big Tom. Thank you, Mike, for driving me around and getting us drunk. Sorry about the Bar Mitzvah thing.

Then, of course, there was David Gentille and Frank Goldstein, my buds. We were in about five of seven classes at Pines Middle school together. We played sports, chased girls, drank wine coolers and beers. We grew up together. You were both nicer and Godlier than I was. Thank you,

for being an example in so many ways, for putting up with me, and being patient and kind enough to be my friend.

Then there was Danny Dominic. He was the little brother I always wanted. And Dave too. We were the Three Musketeers for a while. Love you both! Thank you, boys!

There were many others, including Lloyd, Lane, Angelo, Reece, Dunny, Cuzzy, Amy, Steffi, and Sai.

 INTRODUCE OTHERS

Introducing people to each other is such a simple concept and it is second nature to me. It's amazing how many people skip opportunities to bring strangers together. I believe I was fortunate in learning this behavior very early on in life. Growing up in the restaurant business, I was taught certain social courtesies such as this one. Looking

LIVING WITH JOY, PEACE, AND HAPPINESS

back, I am proud of the fact that I have played a role in building certain friendships by introducing some friends to other friends, who now have become like family to each other as well as to me. Then groups of friends develop and the sense of togetherness and community expands. This is an absolute WIN-WIN! In some cases, I have helped two people who actually had a disdain for each other become close long-term friends. That can't help but make me feel good about making a positive impact on others and the Universe. In one special case, I actually played matchmaker with my boss lady whose beloved husband passed away. I started the ball rolling for her and a regular customer of ours. They played golf together, got engaged, and then married. Hopefully, I helped them have a more fulfilled existence together.

I have also been in situations where I just knew that two people would greatly appreciate each other. Why not give the slight shove needed to create an amazing, heartfelt, momentous experience for two people? For example, we were having a special night in town. The setting was a big birthday party involving a legendary Rock 'n' Roll Hall of Fame drummer. It was a beautiful backdrop for what turned into a gorgeous night and a wonderful memory for so many of us. Early in the night, a Boston musician, who often played for us at the bar, showed up. He was going to open up for the legendary drummer, Artemus Pyle, and his band. I knew it was a big deal for him, like it was for us. We were pumped and excited about the entire evening. Then I ran into an old gentleman from Boston. I knew that he had a historic past as a Vietnam war hero from that town. We were in the parking lot pre-gaming when it dawned on me that these two old school "Bostonites" with two generations in between their ages likely would appreciate comparing notes about their hometown. I introduced the retired Colonel to the thirty-something musician. To say they hit it off is a huge understatement. Within a few minutes, they were taking pictures and exchanging hugs, stories, and phone numbers. I got to watch their joyful reminiscing, proud that I had set that ball rolling in a wonderful direction that had us all feeling SPECIAL.

TRY BELIEVING IN EARTH ANGELS

The first time I ever picked up a hitchhiker was with my friend Andrew in between Los Angeles and Las Vegas back about thirty years ago. Andrew had dated my sister in high school. My sister is still a very attractive lady. Many guys, including several of my good friends, were constantly chasing after her. Andrew was the first guy she dated that I really liked. We bonded quickly and, when they broke up, I think I was more upset about it than she was. He and I became close friends and so I invited him on a trip to Los Angeles and Las Vegas with me. I had moved out west, to L.A., but that stay had lasted only a couple months and then moved back. I wanted to go back for fun, so Andrew agreed to come along.

At the airport on our way out there, Andrew bought a modern version of the Bible. I was completely non-religious and non-believing in God then. Andrew informed me that day that he had recently found God. I congratulated him as sincerely as a non-believer can, and mostly forgot about it. Several days later, we left Vegas and made our way back to L.A. for the last couple days of the trip. We had lost all our cash on a silly, fun romp. On the drive in our rental car, for some strange reason, I stopped to pick up this guy. I remember clearly that he had long blond hair, faded blue jeans, and a

LIVING WITH JOY, PEACE, AND HAPPINESS

plain white undershirt. He looked kind of like a California surfer dude.

I remembered only parts of this story until St. Andrew, as I now think of him, filled in many blanks over the last couple years. Back on that special day, the guy told us that he was an Angel. I remember almost teasing Andrew by saying something like, "I'm sure this is very big for you," since he had just found God and then some guy we picked up claims to be an **ANGEL!** Andrew and I hadn't spoken much of that particular incident over the years, although we remained close. My brother got even closer to him because they ended up rooming together and working together. It started to dawn on me how integral he had been in my life and in the lives of my brother and sister, as well. He was almost like an ANGEL himself, to my family, at least.

So, a couple of years ago, while I was visiting Andrew at his place, he started to fill in the gaps from thirty years before. He reminded me how mean I was to that angel guy that day. He told me how I even teased him after he used his food stamps to buy us food. He then pointed out that I was actually the one to automatically decide to pick the guy up. Andrew had been surprised by that move because I had generally been closed off in many ways. I immediately felt ashamed of the younger me for acting that way towards this kind soul. The person I am today would be totally grateful. I am proud of that change, but I am embarrassed by my behavior back then. St. Andrew was teaching me now that I was receptive to listening and learning.

Andrew went on to inform me that he had not just found God before the L.A. trip, but that he actually discovered God on the first day of that trip! He then said that he believed that my invitation for the trip directly led to him becoming "born again."

This thought, though extremely challenging to digest, slowly sank in and made me feel SPECTACULAR! I now **FULLY BELIEVE that the gentleman hitchhiker we picked up WAS, IN FACT, AN ANGEL.**

For a moment after putting this all together, I was slightly dismayed that it had taken me thirty years longer than Andrew to find GOD, PEACE, JOY, and CLARITY. Any negatives quickly disappeared and were replaced by the REALIZATION that I had found them all finally and that's all that mattered.

I come across so many people daily who are bogged down with their own stresses and worries over minimal problems that are mostly beyond their control. Knowing that I have gotten past that, with the help of GOD and his many Angels, gives me daily peace in knowing that, at the very least, I'm heading in the right direction. Now that I have committed to being a servant of God, I do think of myself as a young Angel recruited by God and his Angels to **SPREAD PEACE, LOVE AND JOY TO EVERYONE.**

LIVING WITH JOY, PEACE, AND HAPPINESS

 ## THE MUSIC OF OUR LIVES

In recent years, my connection with music, and often with specific songs, has increased significantly. I spoke of the **WALK,** when Billy Currington's song, *God Is Great, Beer Is Good And People Are Crazy*, confirmed my **AGREEMENT WITH GOD.** This was just one of many times when the music seemed to convey messages from the Lord. There are so many others now. There are songs I have heard for almost fifty years that never necessarily made sense or impacted me and now resound in an absolutely clear and concise manner. The song, *Let It Be,* is a perfect example. I always loved the song, was moved by it, and also inspired. Then, just a couple of years ago, while I was reconnecting with the Beatles, the Beach Boys, Bob Marley, and some other sixties icons, I caught a little documentary that explained how Paul came up with the song. He describes a dream he had where his mother, Mary, came to him in a dream, **speaking words of wisdom, *LET IT BE.***

I had the realization that my beloved **NANA** was my version of this amazing rock in my life with her words, "**This too shall pass.**" Now, the gorgeous, inspiring, magical song is a tribute to my Nana as well as to anyone else's special Angel in life who knows just what to say and when to say it to GUIDE us through the challenges of life. Thank you, GOD, for providing us with these **BUOYS IN LIFE** that give us refuge and peace in the murky waters that we must navigate on our journey.

Another example of how music affects us and becomes a part of us was shown to me through my relationship with my father. He died over twenty years ago from ALS, or Lou Gherig's Disease. Dad did not talk a lot about God or religion, but he did make it known that he believed firmly in reincarnation and that he wanted to be cremated. As he got closer to dying, he spoke more frequently about the fact that he was going to come back to communicate with us in some way. I became a little more open to the idea of reincarnation then and even read a couple books about **Near Death Experiences** and other phenomena connected with the Afterlife. Then, after his passing, there were many experiences of what I now call those UNIVERSAL CONFIRMATIONS where songs seem to be coming from my dad, Stefan.

For instance, the song, *The Cat's In The Cradle*, by Harry Chapin**,** was a huge song for our family while I was growing up and beyond. My mother informed us that this was the one song that would make my father cry. It was partly because of the beautiful words penned in the poem by Harry's wife that became this huge hit in the seventies. Also, it turned out that my father had attended Cornell University in Ithaca, N.Y. at the same time as Mr. Chapin, so it was extra special to Dad, and then became especially meaningful to us kids. When Dad actually passed, and I was there at the house, the Hospice lady came into the room I was in to inform me. I then called my brother, who lived only a couple of miles away to share the news. He took the short drive over and, in that five-to-seven-minute ride, *The Cat's In The Cradle* **played on his car radio!** There is no way that I can call that a coincidence. Over the twenty-plus years since his death,

LIVING WITH JOY, PEACE, AND HAPPINESS

that song and a couple of others have come on at the most amazing times for me and the family.

One day in the last few years, I was thinking of Dad, when I was contemplating in the shower, of course, whether he had been successful in REACHING US from the other side, as he had promised. After I pondered this question, I then came out of the shower and took a nap on the couch. When I woke up, Pandora on my cell phone was playing the second most meaningful song with him, **Father and Son**, by Cat Stevens, I was thoroughly impressed; you might even say stunned. Then, as I thought he probably did reach us, I put together the other pieces. There is a video of Dad on the MDA telethon, where he literally says, "I'm coming to reach them through my CATS." Then I realized that the songs that reach me the most these days are a song with CATS in the title and one sung by a guy named CAT! I think Dad has stayed with us pretty darn well. Thank you, Daddy! I LOVE YOU!

HINTS 4 HAPPINESS

(Journal break — June, 2020)
The other night in Daytona Beach, an amazing night was had because there was a respect and understanding between us all. Covid had rocked our world. Restaurants, bars, and so much else had closed down. Now while driving up through the state of Florida, I missed out on seeing friends along the way, because I had developed a cough that I knew made people nervous. Now, on this night in Daytona, some bars were starting to slowly open again. It felt like I was there for the unofficial reopening of the town. There was a fun spirit that prevailed. I made a connection with most of the people I talked with because I viewed them with respect and appreciation for just being another human being. There was trust and caring among us all.

IT WAS A BEAUTIFUL, MEMORABLE NIGHT WITH A BUNCH OF "STRANGERS," WHOM I INSTANTLY LOVED AND WILL NEVER FORGET.

 FINDING, EXPERIENCING & LIVING IN HAPPINESS

Here is the challenge I put on myself for these final words:

To leave you with the best chance possible to find, understand, marinate, and live thoroughly in a constant, joyous, peacefully

content place, as I do, and as a blessed and growing population of SPIRITUAL SEEKERS are showing is possible. Here is my final summation of HINTS FOR HAPPINESS. If I've explained everything properly, then these final notes should be something for you to refer to often to keep you on this amazing, magical, adventurous path to HAPPINESS!

CHOOSE HAPPINESS EVERY DAY

Happiness is not only a choice that can be made daily and throughout each day, but it is also a skill to cultivate and can be mastered to experience joy, peace, contentment, and **HAPPINESS!** If you make this a TOP PRIORITY every day, you will achieve it and live it, like I do.

BE GRATEFUL For EVERYTHING

Nothing is guaranteed from your next meal, next paycheck, next friend, next day…down to your next BREATH. Remember that over 200,000 people DIE every day. This is why I thank GOD EVERY MORNING for another day to EXPERIENCE LIFE.

FORGIVE EVERYONE

Keeping anger and feelings of victimization hurts you far more than it likely affects your enemy. I have heard it said that "hate corrodes the container it's held in." The best you can do for yourself, anyone else involved, and the UNIVERSE as a whole, is to do like *Frozen* and LET IT GO! If you can learn to live in "compassionate oneness" and you can stop blaming others and wish EVERYONE well, then you will no longer have need for enemies. The next thing you know, you will be beloved by your community, and this is priceless. This feeling of CONNECTION is HEAVENLY.

HINTS 4 HAPPINESS

DON'T PLAY THE BLAME GAME

Blame only causes pain! Somehow, we have become a society of finger-pointers. It is as much a universal pastime as complaining, and just as much of a waste of energy and time. This trait is what the news and politics are based upon. If you focus on either, or as many do, both, you will notice that this trait is the underlying concept. Who did what? To whom? And then we judge how wrong they are, intimating that WE ARE BETTER! But, once again, who among us is perfect? Who are we to constantly criticize, blame and complain about how others act, when we are far from perfect. So many people live in turmoil, discomfort and frustration, based on what others do, which often has almost nothing to do with them. It's just a way of lashing out for our inner unhappiness. I know that I am exactly where I am in life because of my personal actions and choices, so why would I blame others for ANYTHING?

USE DAILY REMINDERS

Zig Ziglar, the late, great, motivational speaker, author, and sales coach used to tell about how his friend commented on his always reading his positive psychology books. His friend asked, "Weren't you reading that book yesterday, too?" Ziglar's response was, "I took a shower yesterday, too, but I'm going to take another one today."

I have been the same way since I discovered Anthony Robbins at about eighteen years of age. I am always reading about psychology, philosophy, biographies, or other self-help-type non-fiction. I have had this ongoing thirst for knowledge in these areas and I believe that over thirty-five years of such study has given me some long searched for CLARITY. In addition, these readings and now viewings on YouTube or other media act as constant reminders for me to be the person I want to be. Many of us probably feel this way, just for making it past fifty years of age. Understanding how we want to behave or react in life to create the loving environment we desire is one thing. This awareness is a huge step on the path to JOY and HAPPINESS! Even more important to achieving this life that we want where we are living CONGRUENTLY with our true values, is to keep these thoughts near our daily consciousness, so our actions exhibit only these beliefs.

So, for instance, these are the **5 DAILY REMINDERS**:
(I review these in the shower each morning.)

1. ENJOY THE DAY, THE BILL MURRAY WAY
This concept is such a simple one that too often is overlooked. We set goals for everything, but shouldn't having a nice, peaceful, fun, enjoyable experience be one of the most important hopes for the day? I have become a bigger fan of Bill Murray, because of his desire to shake up the monotony of life for himself and others. I strive to do this as well, so "sleepwalking people" can get a glimpse of having fun, just **FOR THE FUN OF IT!**

2. BE HERE NOW, SHOW THE MONKEY BRAIN HOW
Once again, here is insight from Ram Dass, Sadghuru, Wayne Dyer, Eckhart Tolle, and so many others. Don't fret about the future. Don't regret the past. Just BE grateful to BE HERE RIGHT NOW! Showing the MONKEY BRAIN HOW, refers to the Eastern philosophy of quieting your mind. I accomplish this through meditating and also just **STOPPING** and allowing MY mind to rest, with NO THOUGHTS. This takes practice, of course, but once you get better at it, it's priceless to your **POM, PEACE OF MIND.**

HINTS 4 HAPPINESS

3. BE SUPER NICE, LIKE THE 3 B'S AND MR. ROGERS ADVICE

It has come to my attention over the last few years how important kindness is. Because we have become so judgmental of others, we forget this and just get mean. We talk critically about how people look, talk, dress, walk, act, etc. I now realize that **BEING NICE IS THE MOST IMPORTANT THING TO BE.** It's this simple. How do you want to be thought of and eventually remembered? Then live that way, today and EVERYDAY! **EVERYBODY loved, appreciated and admired MR. ROGERS, and he loved everyone.** He is absolutely one of my HEROES. Thank you, Mr. Rogers, for being our friend, our conscience, and our example.

4. BE LIKE THE BUDDHA, AND LIFE WILL BE GOODA! (OR GOUDA)

The Buddha is one of my mentors for sure. The principles of controlling one's own mind have absolutely changed my life and allowed me to live with joy, peace and equanimity. I strive to be like the Buddha each day and I believe life is far better because of it.

5. JUST BE _____

The magical town I live in, Banner Elk, N.C., has been called the B-EZ, and one of the town slogans is to JUST BE, utilizing the town's initials within. And, of course, it refers to the spiritual calmness of JUST BE-ING, in the MOMENT, similar to the concept of BE HERE NOW, but also refers to the go with the flow attitude that many of us have adopted. Then the blank part is another way of looking within and knowing where I need most improvement. So, I will often add a word or phrase to JUST BE, such as, patient, friendly, complimentary, helpful, nicer, etc.

ALL OF THESE ACT AS REMINDERS TO DO BETTER…**CANI!**

LIVING WITH JOY, PEACE, AND HAPPINESS

HAVE FUN, EVERYDAY!

Isn't this one of the main reasons we're here? Now that I have gotten to know GOD, I am confident in saying that **HE** wants us to live with joy, exuberance and yes, FUN! If you have children or pets of any kind, have you ever experienced a moment of watching them in pure joy? Maybe it was their first time frolicking in snow or learning to swim. That moment where you feel the joy as much as or even more than they do. This is how God feels when He sees us LIVE IN THE MOMENT! I believe this is what we ARE HERE FOR!

There is that saying, "Life is not about the amount of moments we breathe, but the moments that take our breath away!"

Life is all about MOMENTS. My definition of these MOMENTS is **when you are awakened by a feeling of significance in a snapshot of time, caused by a profound connection with others or nature, which evokes great emotion, nourishes your soul, and makes you think – this is what life is all about!**

I wish for you, and for everyone, many MOMENTS in life and far fewer stressful times. You CAN CREATE this type of life, by not taking life so seriously. SMILE MORE, LAUGH ALOT, **LIVE FULLY!**

TELL YOUR COMPLAINTS TO YOUR CAT, DOG, HAMSTER, OR SNAKE!

Do you enjoy listening to people complain about their wife, husband, boss, coworker, their health or other issues, or their money woes? The answer for most people is HECK NO! If you're honest with yourself, you will REALIZE that nobody really wants to hear and get drained by this NEGATIVITY. There are those people that we all tend to avoid because they are chronic complainers. I call those people "cloudy all the time." If we become the creator and director of our own lives, then just like a good pilot avoids these dark clouds in the sky, we can dodge and even almost eliminate these negative beings in our lives. Some friends call them "energy vampires," because they can be so exhausting. So, if you can't think of anyone like that, then ask yourself if you are one of them. I was for many years. Now, I CONSCIOUSLY CHOOSE not to be one. I'm pretty sure I've become the total OPPOSITE! So, do you think I'm HAPPIER now or before? I'm fairly confident that I'm more pleasant to be around.

JUST CHOOSE LOVE over EVERYTHING ELSE…over fear, over judgment, and, most of all, over hate.

GIVE, GIVE, GIVE…Of YOURSELF, OF YOUR TIME…GIVE ANYTHING THAT YOU HAVE ENOUGH OF, THAT OTHERS COULD BENEFIT FROM…AND I PROMISE WITH ALL MY MIGHT AND LIGHT …THAT YOU WILL BE HAPPY-ER!

AND…

GUESS what happens to those who suddenly realize that they actually have everything they need and more.

THEY LIVE HAPPILY EVER AFTER!

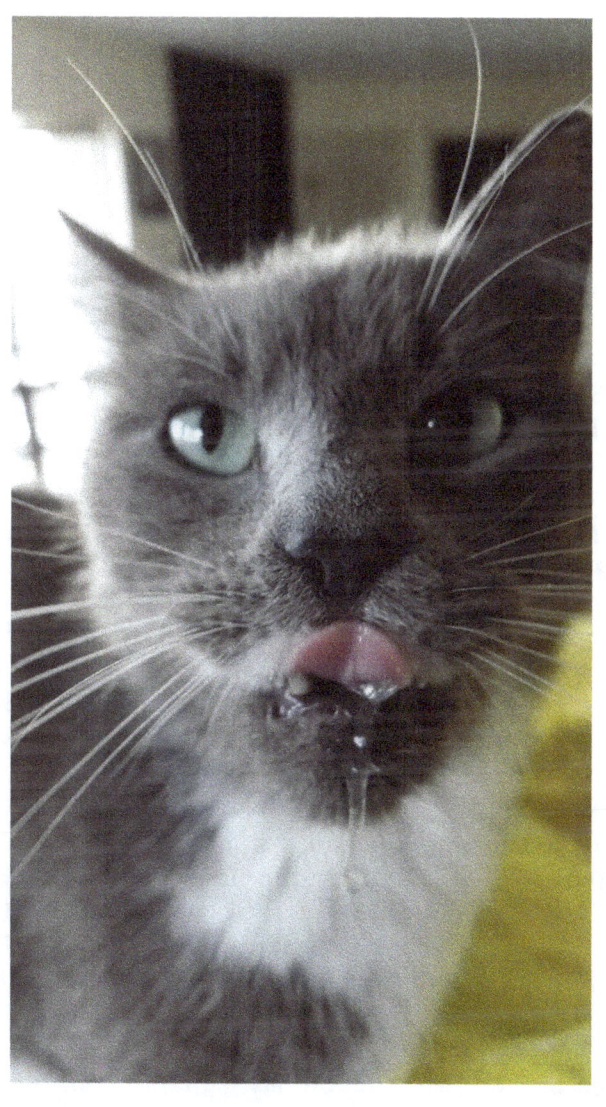

If only we could learn to love more like Joey and Jonathan...
Just imagine...
What a wonderful world this could be!!!

Acknowledgments

I have thanked many people throughout these pages who have meant so much to me on this amazing journey. I would like to add a few more who have been there for me.

My Aunt Judy, Mom's sister, has been like a second mother to me, always encouraging and caring for me endearingly. Thank you. Her first husband Steven was the "fun uncle" growing up, organizing and participating in neighborhood ball games in Scranton that were wonderful. Aunt Judy later married Steve, not to be confused with Steven. The newer uncle Steve was always great to me, and I enjoyed many deep discussions about so many different topics.

Aunt Judy's son JONATHAN is the most special person in my life to this day. It's no coincidence that he is considered "special needs" by the politically correct terminology that is now accepted. Growing up, I got to witness the adventure of all the different schools and living situations that JONATHAN advanced through. My bond with him seems to have been instant and beyond deep. Words cannot properly describe the love and pride I feel for him. I cherish any and all moments with this angel. I truly believe that he has and continues to teach me far more than I could ever teach him. The name JONATHAN means "gift from God" in Hebrew and there is no better way to describe my cousin. I love you beyond words, Jon.

Jonathan's brother Brian was adorable, fun and sweet growing up. We weren't as close as Jon and I were back in the day, well partly because almost nobody was. We have since grown far closer because of our mutual love and caring for Jonathan. Now that we have our priceless, momentous, yearly Eagles road game adventure, I am exceedingly grateful that we have gotten to know each other. I am thoroughly proud of his accomplishments in his field and the generally good person, husband, father, brother and cousin that he had become. Love you, Bri!

My cousin Jason, whom I lovingly refer to as cousin Screech, has become one of my closest friends, confidants and mentors in life and on my spiritual journey. He had peace, calmness and wisdom before I seemed to learn some of my own. He has been THERE FOR ME, as much if not more than anybody else. I am truly grateful for our incredible relationship, thank you, Cuz. Also thank you to cousin Stacy and Aunt Tony for your wonderful presence in my life over the years. Uncle Richard and cousin Jen, too!

Thank you Grandma and Grandpa Stampler for your love, encouragement, guidance and folded up hundreds that you handed me over all those years. Thanks as well for the lovely golfing experiences and dinners at the amazing Mario's in Lauderdale.

I have talked about my perfect Nana and her impact on us and everyone she encountered. I must also give a shout out to her husband, our grandfather, who we called Pop. He was certainly a character with strong personality traits. He was STAUNCH and LOVING. He truly adored spending time with his grandkids and other family. We had many wonderful times together from golf and bowling to many special holidays.

My older brother Russ and I didn't always see eye to eye. I don't know many brothers who have. Underlying any differences we may have had over the years, we have a mutual deep love that only brothers can truly enjoy. He has always been there if I really needed him and I've tried to return that loyalty. I love, respect and appreciate you, Bro! Thank you.

My younger sister Kim and I had a very close and special relationship at certain times throughout life. Then, of course, we had some ups and downs. Her laughter is one of the most beautiful sounds I know. I'm very glad that we have become close again, and it's been awesome watching her two sons, Noah and Brayden, grow into fine young men. It's also been inspiring watching her and my great guy brother-in-law Brett care for each other through the challenges that marriage and family can offer. Thank you all Zaroffs for being there for me and putting up with my changes and weirdness. Love y'all!

Also my brother's two beautiful daughters, Sara and Jenna, have added joy to all our lives. I'm proud of you both. I'm sorry I wasn't around very much over the years, but I love you both dearly. New family members Tom, Pagan, Penny Love and Charly, love you all.

Thank you also to these people who crossed my path and had a positive impact on my life:

Uncle Dave, thanks for showing me the local "ropes" and introducing me to all your "family."

Subway Jimmy, thanks for being a "new" friend and awesome addition to the crew.

Cousin Gary, thank you for being you. You are family.

Sensei Owl Bob, thanks for being there at a perfect time in my journey. Thanks for sharing your stories, insight and wisdom.

A Timeless Treasures Publication.
www.TimelessTreasuresStudio.net

www.ingramcontent.com/pod-product-compliance
Lightning Source LLC
Chambersburg PA
CBHW081132170426
43197CB00017B/2839